Formula 1

technical analysis
2010/2011

The 2010 season will most certainly be remembered as the most exciting from the sporting point of view, as well as the most technically interesting in the recent history of Formula 1. No fewer than five drivers won at least one race (Vettel, Webber, Alonso, Hamilton and Button) in three different cars (Red Bull, Ferrari and McLaren) with the world championship being decided in the thrilling last race of the year. More than anything else – and this is the aspect of most interest to this book – it was a season with a wealth of new developments. The number of new features fielded by the various teams was even superior to those of 2009, despite the regulation earthquake generated by the Federation. This further regulation tremor banning refuelling had the effect of re-shuffling the cards and fully stimulating the designers' imaginations.

Despite controversy over the diffusers, the 2009 season had already been the most interesting of recent years and the stimulating effect did not dim in 2010: in fact, it infected everyone, even the teams that were not very daring the previous year, interpretations of the regulations apart. Although without double diffusers, Red Bull immediately looked like the most innovative car of the last 20 years. But just about every car had some new or

even revolutionary feature or other in 2010. Liberalising the concept of the hole to feed double (if not triple) central diffusers, designers went even further and came up with not only aerodynamics but the whole car built around this concept. Ferrari did not hide its intentions at the end of the 2009 season. "To have a really efficient double diffuser you have to redesign everything", one prominent member of its technical team said. And that is what happened: they not only designed a long fuel tank, but also an all-new, longer gearbox. Then came brilliance: they inclined the engine-gearbox group to gain even more space around the mechanics, in part because the 'box was decidedly narrower. Red Bull achieved the same objective by slightly raising the transmission, and that was longer and narrower, too. But the two great technical concepts that set trends during the 2010 season came from McLaren and Red Bull. The former the F-duct – that was what it was generally called, even if McLaren called it the F-flap.

The second was the exhausts blowing into the diffusers. Another new solution was the one brought in by Mercedes-Benz, with a safety roll bar shaped like a narrow pyramid. It was one of Ross Brawn's deft moves that made way for the modification of the air intake without having to be subjected to another crash test. Strangely, this new feature then became an obstacle to the introduction of the F-duct, because that never married well with a fin shaped engine cover. It was from that situation that the complicated and less efficient solution was created by the Stuttgart team, which we shall describe in the New Solutions chapter.

A SEASON OF EVEN MORE DEVELOPMENTS

There were not only new developments at the start of the year: the 2010 season took place with a race to pursue the two key features thrown into the ring by McLaren and Red Bull. All the other teams had to devote more

Red Bull RB6

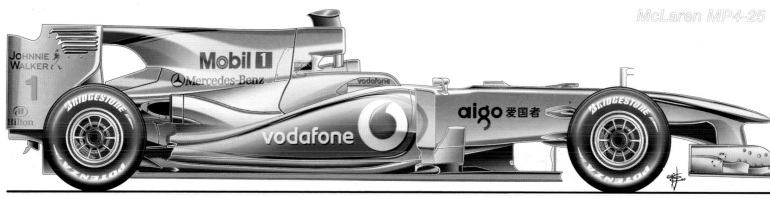

McLaren MP4-25

energy and money to those two projects, complicating and enriching the development logic of their cars to adapt them to the characteristics of the various circuits.

To that was added that, never more than in the 2010 season, there were so many revolutionary cars; not only between the Thursday and Friday but even between the two practice sessions of the same day.

Often, components in extremis were fitted to a car at the last moment without having covered a single test kilometre, which was also caused by the abolition of private testing; that forced the teams to transform the Friday into a real test session for subsequent races.

The introduction of the F-duct and exhaust blow often took place over a number of attempts before their definitive use in races. Ferrari were extremely good at achieving their objective immediately, especially with the blow into the diffusers, and that enabled them to take an important step forward right from their debut at Valencia.

HIGH COSTS

The development of the exhaust blow was one of the most expensive technical initiatives of recent years.

The tremendous heat of over 600°C generated by the exhausts, the blow from which was purposely directed towards the diffusers' lateral channels, literally roasted the aerodynamic devices.

So the teams had to coat them with a new substance called pyrossic, a mix of ceramic material, glass and resin produced by one single factory in Europe, with its headquarters in France.

The cost of this latest technical sophistication sent minds spinning: it was around £1 million Sterling, of which £200,000 was for the production of the exhausts, £300,000 for bench tests and their tuning to the engine's characteristics, plus £100,000 for the construction of at least five of the new diffusers.

The rest was taken up by wind tunnel testing and CFD systems calculations.

CONTROVERSIES

There were no major controversies during the 2010 season: the question of the F-duct was immediately resolved with the consent of the Federation, which balked any other countermove. But there was often a little ill humour going around about the missile-like performance of the Red Bulls and lack of respect for the budget cuts decided by FOTA members. FIA's Charlie Whiting sometimes had to intervene without disqualifications to block certain interpretations, such as that of the starter hole, which in some teams (McLaren, Mercedes-Benz, Renault and Force India) had become a further element of blow in the central channels of the diffusers. Especially at the GP of Turkey, where Adrian Newey had to modify no fewer than five details on the Red Bulls, the most important regarding the rear suspension pull rod link that did not respect the dimensional limits imposed by the regulations.

Then there was the abolition of the mirrors fitted to the turning vanes in front of the side-

Ferrari F10

Mercedes MGP W01

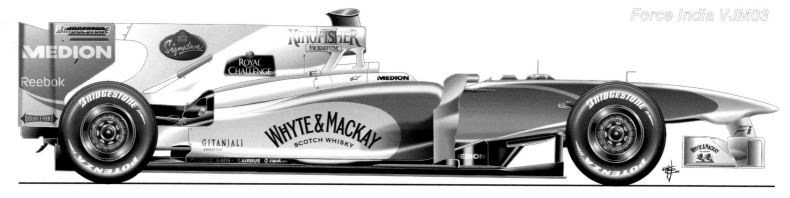

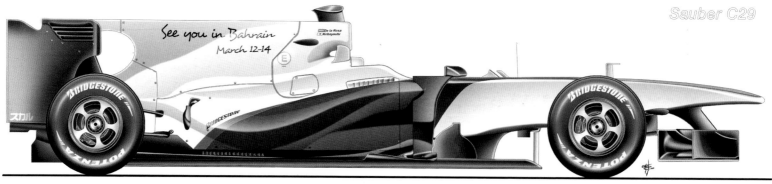

See you in Bahrain
March 12-14

pods, a long way from the cockpit and the drivers' sight. It was a decision dictated by safety reasons and, therefore, came into immediate effect from the GP of Spain. The increased traffic with 24 cars on the circuit – at least six of them very slow – imposed this decision so that seven of the 12 teams competing for the 2010 world championship had to bring their cars into line. They were Ferrari, Red Bull, Sauber, Williams, Force India, Toro Rosso and Hispania Racing. And finally, there was the case of the Red Bulls' front wing, which television pictures showed was clearly flexing – as was that of the Ferrari, but less so – especially at the GP of Hungary although it brilliantly passed tech-

nical scrutineering: the Federation decided that the scrutineering procedure would be modified from the GP of Belgium.
A more severe test for the bib splitter under the chassis (as you will see in the 2010 Regulations chapter) came into force at the subsequent Italian GP at Monza, putting an end to that controversy.

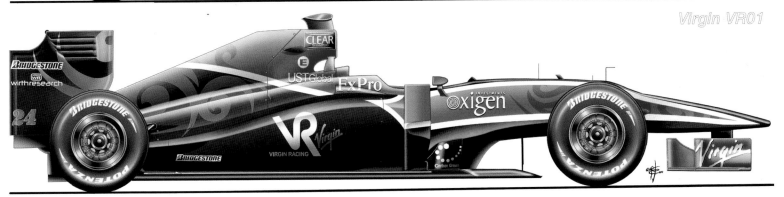

NEW TEAMS

With the retirement of the two major car manufacturers BMW and Toyota, three new teams joined the Circus, Lotus, Virgin and HRT with all their cars powered by 'new' Cosworth engines. Despite the fact that Mike Gascoyne's Lotus turned out to be superior to the other two, these cars reached a level of competitiveness that was almost equal to the GP2 competitors. And not one of them distinguished itself by coming up with an interesting solution. Virgin even had to rebuild its chassis for the GP of Spain, because of the clamorous mistake that was made on the dimensions of its fuel tank.

The 2010 'Technical Analysis of Formula 1' has once more benefitted from a contribution of Franco Nugnes for the Engines chapter; engineer Giancarlo Bruno for Suspensions and Tyres; engineer Kazuhito Kasai also for Tyres. Special thanks go to Paddy Lowe (McLaren), Sam Michael (Williams) and engineer Mauro Piccoli (Brembo) for the data they supplied for the respective chapters.

ue to parc fermé, the car park where the F1 cars remained between qualifying and the race that was introduced in 2008, and the abolition of the use of the spare cars, the usual graphs that revealed interesting details in the past became more linear.

Among the 2010 top teams, only Ferrari reassembled a spare, naked monocoque for a race. It happened at Monaco, when Fernando Alonso damaged his car irreparably during practice.

Among other things, the regulations do not permit a driver to participate in the subsequent practice session on the same day after an accident.

For that reason, the reserve monocoque had to be completely bare and not pre-assembled, as happened in previous seasons to speed up the replacement operation.

RED BULL

The team that built the most chassis was Red Bull with seven, followed by Ferrari with six, Mercedes-Benz and Renault with five and a large group which, surprisingly, included McLaren with four; Williams, Sauber, Force India, Toro Rosso, Lotus constructed the same number.

The group ends with HRT's three chassis, while Virgin had to build three plus another two "simply" because the technical group directed by Nick Wirth made a mistake with the fuel tank capacity and they were forced to construct another two for the Grand Prix of Spain.

Chassis F10	First run 2010	Km completed GP	Km completed TEST
281	20 GEN	3.144,7	8.045
282	15 FEB	1.794.8	6.850,1
283	25 FEB	3.933,5	8.207,5
284	01 MAG	9.921,6	10.267,4
285	18 GIU	8.739,7	2.060
286	24 SET	1.183,6	1.258,4

RED BULL • *RB7* • N° 5-6

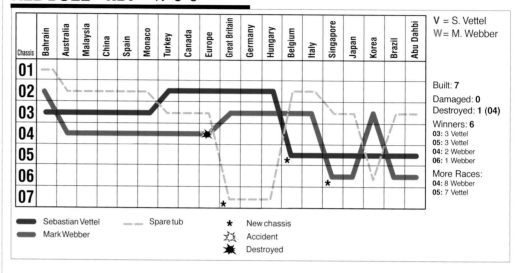

V = S. Vettel
W = M. Webber

Built: **7**
Damaged: **0**
Destroyed: **1 (04)**

Winners: **6**
03: 3 Vettel
05: 3 Vettel
04: 2 Webber
06: 1 Webber

More Races:
04: 8 Webber
05: 7 Vettel

━━ Sebastian Vettel ╌╌ Spare tub ★ New chassis
━━ Mark Webber ✳ Accident ✴ Destroyed

McLAREN • *MP4-25* • N° 1-2

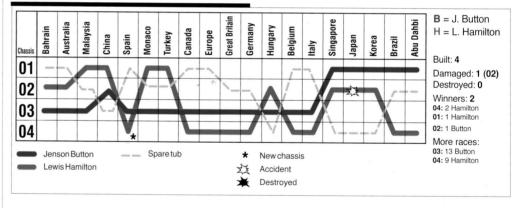

B = J. Button
H = L. Hamilton

Built: **4**
Damaged: **1 (02)**
Destroyed: **0**

Winners: **2**
04: 2 Hamilton
01: 1 Hamilton
02: 1 Button

More races:
03: 13 Button
04: 9 Hamilton

━━ Jenson Button ╌╌ Spare tub ★ New chassis
━━ Lewis Hamilton ✳ Accident ✴ Destroyed

FERRARI • *F10* • N° 7-8

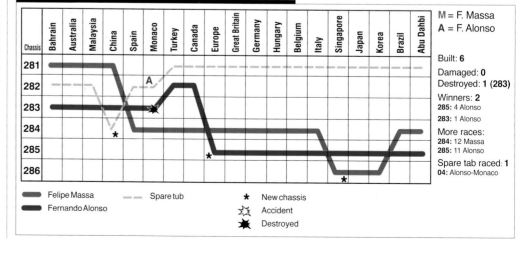

M = F. Massa
A = F. Alonso

Built: **6**
Damaged: **0**
Destroyed: **1 (283)**

Winners: **2**
285: 4 Alonso
283: 1 Alonso

More races:
284: 12 Massa
285: 11 Alonso

Spare tab raced: **1**
04: Alonso-Monaco

━━ Felipe Massa ╌╌ Spare tub ★ New chassis
━━ Fernando Alonso ✳ Accident ✴ Destroyed

ODDITIES

CHASSIS DESTROYED AND INVOLVED IN ACCIDENTS

The number of destroyed chassis was much reduced in 2010: they included one of Red Bull's (Valencia, Webber), one of Ferrari's (Monaco, Alonso), one of Renault's (Korea, Petrov) and one Lotus (Singapore, Kovalainen).

Damaged: Renault one (Korea, Petrov), Mercedes-Benz one (Korea, Rosberg), Force India one (Japan, Liuzzi), Toro Rosso two (Singapore, Alguersuari) and Korea, Buemi).

VICTORIOUS CHASSIS

After a record six victorious teams in 2008 (Ferrari, McLaren, BMW, Toro Rosso and Renault), the number dropped to four in 2009 (Brawn GP, Red Bull, McLaren and Ferrari) and diminished further to just three teams in 2010 (Red Bull, Ferrari and McLaren) after a season that was technically extremely lively and interesting.

The award for the most victories in 2010 goes to Ferrari's chassis number 285 with four wins by Fernando Alonso; that is followed by Red Bull chassis numbers 03 and 05 with three successes each, scored by Sebastian Vettel. Two victories went to both Red Bull chassis 04 with Mark Webber, and the McLaren 04 driven by Lewis Hamilton. A single win was scored by both Red Bull 03 and 06 with Vettel and Webber and McLaren's 01 and 02 with Button and Hamilton and Ferrari's 283 with Alonso.

RENAULT

This team built five chassis, but used only four: in fact, 01 was never taken to a circuit.

PASSO

The longest car was the McLaren at 3,480 mm, followed by Force India (3,411 mm), which used the same engine and, above all, gearbox. Then comes: Sauber, Ferrari, Toro Rosso, Red Bull, Renault, Lotus, Williams, Mercedes-Benz, HRT and Virgin.

RELIABILITY

The most reliable team was Ferrari, having covered an incredible 97.2% of the entire world championship's laps. Second came Red Bull at 93.4%, third Mercedes-Benz (91.3%), followed by McLaren (89.6%). The least reliable team was Sauber, having covered only 67.6% and experiencing four engine breakdowns. The penultimate was Virgin at 70.4%, but with suspensions that broke four times.

	laps completed (%)	finishes	technical failures	accidents
Ferrari	2194 (97,2%)	35	**1** engine	2
Red Bull	2110 (93,4%)	33	**2** loose wheelnut-engine	3
Mercedes	2062 (91,3%)	33	**3** loose wheelnut	2
McLaren	2023 (89,6%)	32	**2** oil leak-gearbox	4
Williams	1951(86,4%)	32	**1** exhaust	5
Toro Rosso	1937 (85,8%)	30	**4** electrics-hydraulics-brakes-engine	4
Renault	1935 (85,7%)	29	**5** gearbox-f. susp.-brakes-driveshaft-loose wheelnut	4
Force India	1834 (81,2%)	27	**4** electrics(2)-ignition(1)-oil leak	6
Lotus	1742 (77,1%)	21	**13** hydraulics(6)-gearbox(3)-steering(2)-brakes(1)-r. wing	0
HRT	1659 (73,5%)*	23	**10** engine(1)-hydraul.(3)-r. susp.(2)gearbox(2)-fuel press(2)	11
Virgin	1591 (70,4%)*	19	**14** hydraul.(5)-susp(4)-gearbox(2)-clutch(1)-engine(1)-l. wheelnut(1)	4
Sauber	1526 (67,6%)*	22	**11** engine(4)-hydraul.(3)-gearbox(2)-susp.(1)-r. wing	5

		5-6 RED BULL	1-2 MCLAREN	7-8 FERRARI	3-4 MERCEDES	11-12 RENAULT
		RB7	**MP4-25**	**F10**	**MGPW01**	**RE30**
CAR	Designers	Adrian Newey Rob Marshall	Jonathan Neale - Neil Oatley Paddy Lowe	Aldo Costa - Nikolas Tombazis Luca Marmorini	Ross Brawn Steve Clark	James Allison
	Race engineers	Giullaume Rocquelin (5) Ciaron Pilbeam (16)	Jakob Andreasen (1) Andy Latham (2)	Rob Smedley (7) Andrea Stella (8)	Jock Clear (4) Andrew Shovlin (3)	Simon Rennie (11) Mark Slade (12)
	Chief mechanic	Kenny Handkammer	Pete Vale	Francesco Ugozzoni	Mattew Deane	Gavin Hudson
CHASSIS	Wheelbase	3295,6 mm*	3480 mm*	3355 mm*	3208 mm*	3320 mm*
	Front track	1440 mm*	1470 mm*	1470 mm	1470 mm	1450 mm
	Rear track	1410 mm*	1405 mm*	1405 mm	1405 mm	1420 mm
	Front suspension	2+1 dampers and torsion bars	2+1 dampers and torsion bars	2+1 dampers and torsion bars	2+1 dampers and torsion bars	2+1 dampers and torsion bars
	Rear suspension	Pull-Rod 2+1 dampers	2+1 dampers and torsion bars	2+1 dampers and torsion bars	2+1 dampers and torsion bars	2+1 dampers and torsion bars
	Dampers	Multimatic	McLaren	Sachs	Sachs	Penske
	Brakes calipers	Brembo	Akebono	Brembo	Brembo	A+P
	Brakes discs	Brembo	Carbon Industrie - Brembo	Brembo CCR Carbon Industrie	Brembo	Hitco
	Wheels	O.Z.	Enkey	BBS	BBS	AVUS
	Radiators	Marston	Calsonic - IMI	Secan	Secan	Marston
	Oil tank	middle position inside fuel tank	middle position inside fuel tank	middle position inside fuel tank	middle position inside fuel tank	middle position inside fuel tank
GEARBOX		Longitudinal carbon	Longitudinal carbon	Longitudinal carbon	Longitudinal carbon	Longitudinal titanium
	Gear selection	Semiautomatic 7 gears	Semiautomatic 7 gears	Semiautomatic 7 gears	Semiautomatic 7 gears	Semiautomatic 7 gears
	Clutch	A+P	A+P	Sachs	Sachs	A+P
	Pedals	2	2	2	2	2
ENGINE		Renault RS27	Mercedes FO108W	Ferrari 056	Mercedes FO108W	Renault RS27
	Total capacity	2398 cmc	2400 cmc	2400 cmc	2400 cmc	2400 cmc
	N cylinders and V	8 - V 90	8 - V 90	8 - V 90	8 - V 90	8 - V 90
	Electronics	Magneti Marelli	McLaren el. sys.	Magneti Marelli	Mercedes	Magneti Marelli
	Fuel	Elf	Mobil	Shell	Mobil	Elf
	Oil	Elf	Mobil	Shell	Mobil	Elf
	Dashboard	Red Bull	McLaren	Magneti Marelli	Mercedes	Renault F1

*Extimated value

Car **TABLE**

9-10 **WILLIAMS**	14-15 **FORCE INDIA**	22-23 **SAUBER**	16-17 **TORO ROSSO**	18-19 **LOTUS**	20-21 **HRT**	24-25 **VIRGIN**
FW32	**WJM03**	**C29**	**STR5**	**T127**	**FRT F110**	**VR-01**
Patrick Head - Sam Michael Ed Wood	Mark Smith	James Key M. Duesmann	Giorgio Ascanelli Ben Butler-Laurent Mekies	Mike Gascoine	Geoff Willis	Nick Wirth
T. Ross (9) Tom McCullough (10)	Bradley Joyce (14) Gianpiero Lambiase (15)	Paul Russell (22) Francesco Nenci (23)	Riccardo Adami (16) Andrea Landi (17)	Gianluca Pisanello (18) Juan Pablo Ramirez (19)	Richard Connell (20) Francisco Javier Pujolar (21)	Dave Greenwood (24) Mark Hutcheson (25)
Carl Gaden	Andy Deeming	Amiel Lindesay	Gerard Lecoq	Phil Spencer	Ernst Kopp	Richard Wrenn
3218 mm	3411 mm*	3371 mm*	3298 mm*	3318 mm*	3249 mm	3183 - 3318 mm*
1480 mm	1480 mm	1460 mm	1440 mm	1470 mm	1425 mm	1440 mm
1420 mm	1410 mm	1400 mm	1410 mm	1405 mm	1411 mm	1410 mm
2+1 dampers and torsion bars	2+1 dampers and torsion bars	2+1 dampers and torsion bars	2+1 dampers and torsion bars	2+1 dampers and torsion bars	2+1 dampers and torsion bars	2+1 dampers and torsion bars
2+1 dampers and torsion bars	2+1 dampers and torsion bars	2+1 dampers and torsion bars	Pull-Rod 2+1 dampers	2+1 dampers and torsion bars	2+1 dampers and torsion bars	Pull-Rod 2+1 dampers
Williams	Sachs	Sachs	Koni	Sachs	Sachs	Koni
A+P	A+P	Brembo	Brembo	A+P	Brembo	A+P
Carbon Industrie	Hitco - Brembo	Brembo	Brembo	Hitco	Brembo	Hitco
O.Z.	BBS	O.Z.	O.Z.	BBS	OZ	BBS
IMI Marston	Secan	Calsonic	Marston	Secan	Secan	Marston
middle position inside fuel tank	middle position inside fuel tank	middle position inside fuel tank	middle position inside fuel tank	middle position inside fuel tank	middle position inside fuel tank	middle position inside fuel tank
Longitudinal titanium	Longitudinal carbon	Longitudinal titanium	Longitudinal carbon	Xtrac Longitudinal	Xtrac Longitudinal	Virgin
Semiautomatic 7 gears	Semiautomatic 7 gears	Semiautomatic 7 gears	Semiautomatic 7 gears	Semiautomatic 7 gears	Semiautomatic 7 gears	Semiautomatic 7 gears
A+P	A+P	A+P	A+P	A+P	A+P	A+P
2	2	2	2	2	2	2
Cosworth CA2010	Mercedes FO108W	Ferrari 056	Ferrari 056	Cosworth CA2010	Cosworth CA2010	Cosworth CA2010
2400 cmc	2400 cmc	2400 cmc	2400 cmc	2400 cmc	2400 cmc	2400 cmc
8 - V 90	8 - V 90	8 - V 90	8 - V 90	8 - V 90	8 - V 90	8 - V 90
-	McLaren el. sys.	Magneti Marelli	Magneti Marelli	-	-	-
Esso	Mobil	-	Shell	Esso	BP	BP
Esso	Mobil	Mobil1	Shell	Esso	BP	BP
Williams	P. I.	Magneti Marelli	Toro Rosso	Williams	Williams	Williams

The Federation opted for stability in 2010 after the raging controversies generated by the revolution introduced the previous year.

The new regulations only demanded three modifications to the technical rules: a minimum weight increase from 605 to 620 kg, the abolition of rim covers and a 0.75 inch reduction in width of the front tyres' tread area. The latter notably changed the cars' weight distribution, moving it by 1-2 points more to the rear with values of around 46%-47% for the fronts.

This time, the big revolution was sparked off by a sporting rule that does not appear in the tech regs: it was the abolition of refuelling, 16 years after it was first introduced. An explosive move, because it completely upset the imposition of the cars, with implications that were not just limited to the design phase but also to many other technical aspects, like the management of the cars and race strategies with a more direct involvement of the drivers in the achievement of the results.

Another sporting norm with serious technical implications was the return of qualifying with all but empty fuel tanks. Yet another variable, because the teams had to make major compromises in the set-up of their cars between qualifying and the race. This because the parc fermé rule remained in force.

Modifications to set-ups were prohibited between qualifying with nearly empty tanks and the race with a full load of petrol.

At the start of a race, the weight of the 2010 cars had become about 787 kg.

Their minimum weight was up to 620 kg plus about 167 kg of fuel at maximum load, against approximately 665 kg in 2009, made up of the regulation 605 kg plus a maximum of about 60 kg of fuel for the first part of the race. The difference in weight between qualifying and the grand prix could, therefore, reach over 160 kg – and that had its effect on set-ups, but more than anything else on the cars' height from the ground.

Tyre changes were not abolished.

During pre-season testing, it was seen that all the teams had worked out ways of speeding up pit stops as much as possible.

But let's look at the change that outlawed refuelling again. Tyre changes took place in less than four seconds.

The cars had become much longer – in some cases more than the 15-20 cm envisaged and indicated in the layout – and with a slightly more substantial central section.

Fuel tank capacity more or less doubled, as it

went from 100-120 litres to around 240 litres.

So obviously, tanks became much longer – about 15 cm, – as there is a constraint of 80 cm in width and it is not all that wise to look for more volume in height. So the only possibility was to accommodate the greater amount of fuel in longer tanks which, in turn, meant longer cars.

One of the modified technical regulations banned rim covers, with the excuse that, having created a dangerous situation in 2009, and they made tyre changes more difficult. This, together with the reduction in the front tyre section, had a major influence on aerodynamic studies of the cars' forward sections.

This time, Ferrari ably got around the prohibition of the rim covers by coming up with wheels which included a ring with an aerodynamic function in their design.

Other small modifications to the tech regs – the result of dangerous situations that had arisen in recent seasons – was the abolition of the manual wheel nut tightener, introduced back in 1995, in favour of an automatic mechanical system elaborated by the various teams.

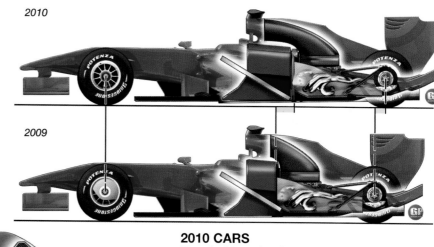

2010

2009

2010 CARS

The abolition of re-fuelling changed the cars' architecture, notably lengthening their wheelbase. In these comparative illustrations are the differences between the 2009 season cars (above) and those of 2010.

1) The front flap rule remained unchanged.

2) The aerodynamic rim covers were abolished for safety reasons during ultra-fast tyre changes of under four seconds. The front tyres are narrower, with a footprint of 240 mm instead of 2009's 270 mm.

4) In practice, the fuel tank's capacity had doubled. It had no alternative but to become a minimum of 15 cm longer. 5) To limit the wheelbase increase, the gearbox became more compact in some cases. 6) The wheelbase increased by around 15-18 cm.

+15 cm

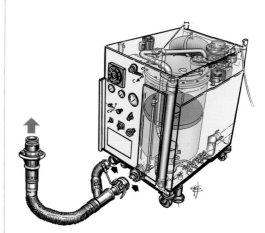

RE-FUELLING ABOLISHED

Introduced in 1994, the abolition of re-fuelling freed the teams' pits of bulky re-fuelling equipment – two units per team – with a considerable transport cost saving.

The illustration shows the voluminous equipment, supplied by Intertechnique of France.

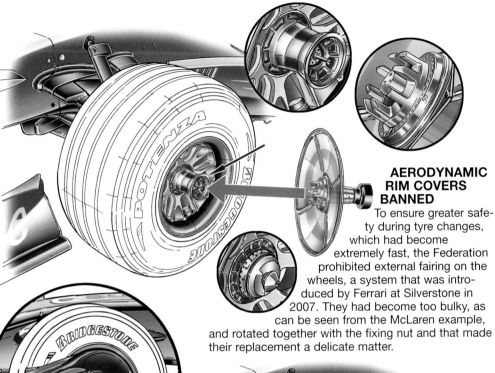

AERODYNAMIC RIM COVERS BANNED

To ensure greater safety during tyre changes, which had become extremely fast, the Federation prohibited external fairing on the wheels, a system that was introduced by Ferrari at Silverstone in 2007. They had become too bulky, as can be seen from the McLaren example, and rotated together with the fixing nut and that made their replacement a delicate matter.

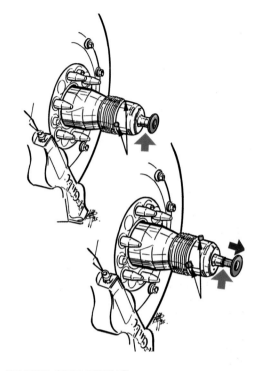

WHEEL NUT FIXING

The 1995 system by which a mechanic manually tightened the wheel nut was also banned to avoid the accidents of the last two years. The Federation imposed an automatic mechanical system on the teams that was faster and safer.
The small blocking tabs exit the base as soon as the air gun is taken away.

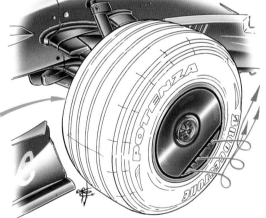

FERRARI RIM

Ferrari proved itself to be extremely able in getting around the abolition of rim covers. It came up with a rim with a ring that played an aerodynamic role.
No other team was able to copy it, because rims are among the components that each team must homologate at the start of the season and they may not be modified.

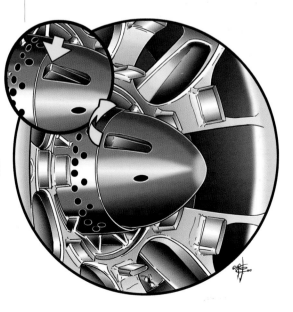

EXTERNAL REAR MIRRORS BANNED

At the second race of the season, the Federation decided to ban the external position of the mirrors for safety reasons with almost immediate effect, from the GP of Spain. The mirrors had been moved to external positions for greater aerodynamic efficiency and appeared first on the 2006 Ferrari, then on most of the other cars. The two illustrations show the 248 F1 and F10 examples, the latter as it appeared in Spain. No fewer than seven of the 12 teams competing for the world championship had to modify the position of their mirrors and they were Ferrari, of course, Red Bull, Sauber, Williams, Force India, Toro Rosso and Hispania Racing.

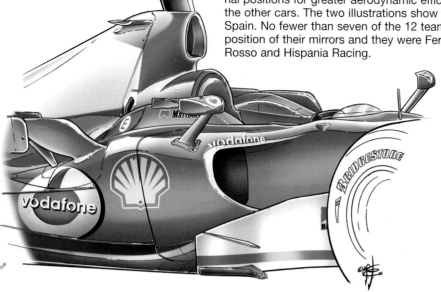

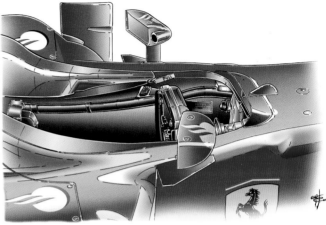

FLEXIBLE FRONT WING

Controversy blew up at the GP of Hungary when it seemed evident from TV pictures just how much the Red Bull front wing flexed at its extremities. It almost touched the ground, a sign that the 50 kg load applied at verification was completely insufficient.

It was only supposed to flex 75 mm in height in relation to the reference plane, so the Federation decided to make front wing flexing checks more severe from the GP of Belgium.

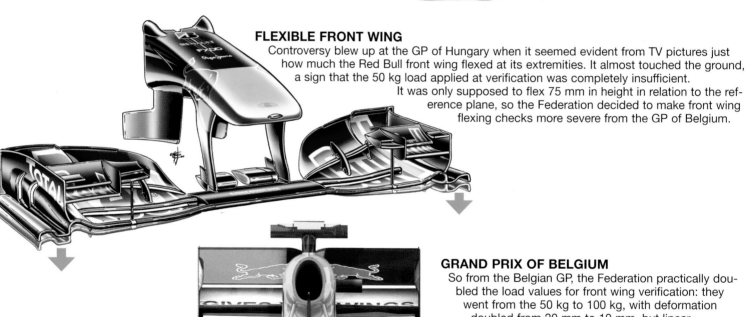

GRAND PRIX OF BELGIUM

So from the Belgian GP, the Federation practically doubled the load values for front wing verification: they went from the 50 kg to 100 kg, with deformation doubled from 20 mm to 10 mm, but linear.

Above all, however, with a greater surface to be controlled, as checks were no longer limited just to its periphery, where the bargeboards are located. It is worth mentioning that F1 measurements are no longer taken in relation to the ground, but to the reference plane, which is the lowest point of the chassis.

100kg
= **(50 kg)**

+75 mm
PR

(10 mm)
20 mm

795 mm

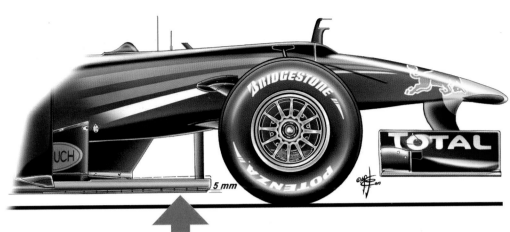

MONZA

A further verification variation was brought in at Monza, this time concerning the shadow plate under the chassis.

The load to which this initial part of the stepped bottom must resist remained unchanged at 200 kg, as did the permitted deformation of 5 mm.

But the test method became more severe and complete as it was no longer carried out at the one single central point, but its two extremities to avoid peripheral deformation. This part, together with the set-up of the car's nose, helps that area to seal itself to the ground for greater aerodynamic efficiency.

200 kg

5 mm ↑

200 kg

SINGAPORE

The subsequent race was the GP of Singapore, where many teams had modified the knife edge zone to make it more rigid.

The easiest mod to see was of the Mercedes-Benz, which doubled the struts in that area.

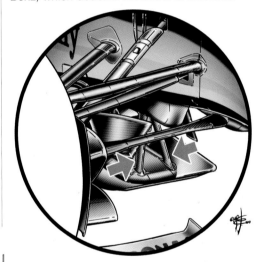

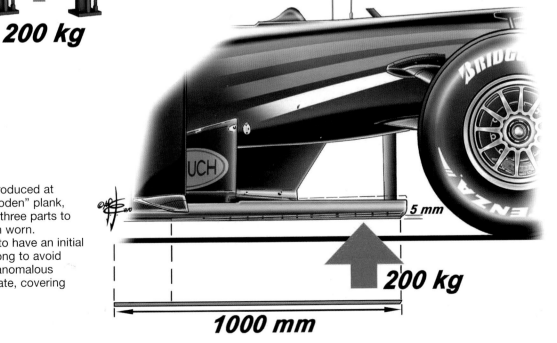

5 mm

200 kg

1000 mm

PLANK

Another new development introduced at Monza was the so-called "wooden" plank, which could be dismantled in three parts to facilitate its replacement when worn.

From the Italian round, it had to have an initial section of at least 1000 mm long to avoid greater flexing in the case of anomalous deformation of the shadow plate, covering about 60-70 cm in length.

The return of another form of technology from the past is down to Adrian Newey, as was the case in 2009 with the rear suspension pull rod layout. At the beginning of 2010, this ingenious technician re-exhumed the lateral blow of the engine's exhausts in front of the rear wheels, which was briefly introduced by Renault's Michel Tetu on the RB60 in 1985, leading to an even more extreme form of exhaust blow in the lateral channels, a re-take of the first blow into the diffusers initially devised by Renault in 1983. It was Jean Claude Migeot, the French company's head of aerodynamics, who masterminded the RE40 at Monaco, with the small exhaust terminals that blew directly into the lateral channels of the diffuser.

That was the year of the major regulation revolution and the abolition of wing planes on the sidepods, as well as the introduction of the flat bottom. From here came the absolute necessity to recover about 80 kg of downforce in the small portion destined for the diffusers in the rear area of the car.

However, this technique embodied a number of negatives, because the weight was all on the rear axle. So there was a great deal of traction coming out of a slow corner but the car was too throttle-sensitive in fast curves, especially on long sections.

That is why Renault often preferred high exhausts, taking into account the circuit concerned and/ or the driver's style. Interestingly, the Renault RE40 was one of the most competitive cars of its period, with Prost ending up just two points from Nelson Piquet, who became that year's world champion in the Brabham. The French company also tried lateral blow on the RE60, taking the opposite direction to that of Adrian Newey, who was the first to bring back this technique on the RB5 from the fourth Grand Prix of the season in Chin, but then the exhausts blew into its lateral channels. That is why the engine, with its development frozen by the Federation, became a further element with which to improve the cars' aerodynamics while respecting what was another regulation revolution sanctioned way back in 1983.

As with all new solutions, the one introduced by Renault was the subject of an official protest by Brabham at the Grand Prix of the United States, held in Detroit: the British team contested the fact that the exhaust blow had become a mobile aerodynamic device and, therefore, was contrary to the spirit of the regulation. The protest was rejected by both the sports commissioners and at the subsequent appeal to the FISA (now FIA) tribunal on 26 July. From that day on, the objective of all the other teams was to adopt a similar solution. As well as the blow into the diffusers, there were also other attempts that were sometimes extravagant, like the really long terminals tested by Rory Byrne on his 1992 Benetton. With the return of normally aspirated engines and drivers having to "play" more with the gas, the value of the downforce determined by the exhaust blow became extremely variable, dependent on the position of the accelerator. In 1998, there was another revolution caused this time by a regulation modification, which considered the exhausts an integral part of the body.

At that year's Grand Prix of Spain, Rory Byrne's Ferrari appeared with exhausts that blew into the upper part of the body, a technique which slowly spread and was retained on F1 cars until the previous season.

But the most important change to this solution, which would otherwise make it part of the aerodynamics chapter, is in the tremendous amount of work carried out by the engine specialists, with those of Renault at the top of the list. They tried to reduce the difference in the aerodynamic "help" between the blow phases with the engine in acceleration and in deceleration. All of that to avoid brusque variations in load between the two situations, which create aerodynamic instability. And that caused the abandonment of the solution for normally aspirated engines at the end of the Eighties.

FERRARI

Ferrari also introduced an exclusive solution for the 2010 season. Their engine (1) was installed at a 3.5° angle (2) to create more space in the double diffuser area. A technique discussed in more detail in the New Developments chapter, but which is relevant here to show how much the power unit was an integral part of the car's aerodynamic package.

RED BULL

Adrian Newey brought back the low blow exhausts idea, which Renault first came up with in 1983. He did so at the beginning of the season with a solution at the sides of the terminal part of the sidepods, but Red Bull arrived in China with a more extreme version that blew into the diffuser's lateral channels (circle). It was a development that had required a great deal of work from the engine specialists.

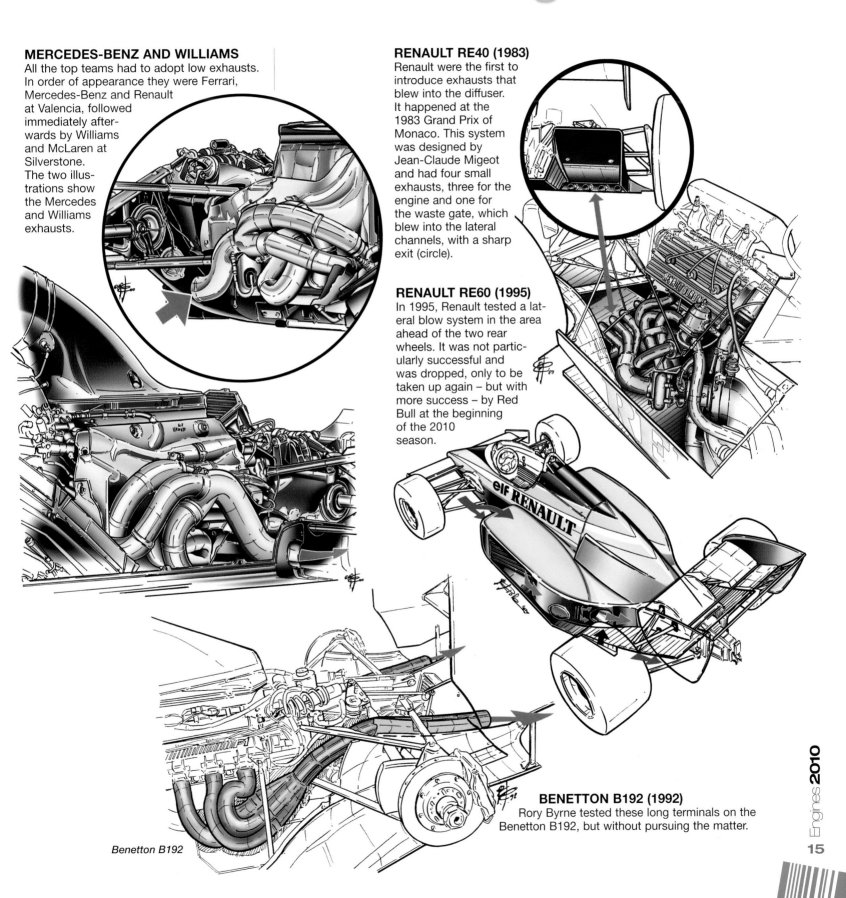

MERCEDES-BENZ AND WILLIAMS
All the top teams had to adopt low exhausts. In order of appearance they were Ferrari, Mercedes-Benz and Renault at Valencia, followed immediately afterwards by Williams and McLaren at Silverstone. The two illustrations show the Mercedes and Williams exhausts.

RENAULT RE40 (1983)
Renault were the first to introduce exhausts that blew into the diffuser. It happened at the 1983 Grand Prix of Monaco. This system was designed by Jean-Claude Migeot and had four small exhausts, three for the engine and one for the waste gate, which blew into the lateral channels, with a sharp exit (circle).

RENAULT RE60 (1995)
In 1995, Renault tested a lateral blow system in the area ahead of the two rear wheels. It was not particularly successful and was dropped, only to be taken up again – but with more success – by Red Bull at the beginning of the 2010 season.

BENETTON B192 (1992)
Rory Byrne tested these long terminals on the Benetton B192, but without pursuing the matter.

Benetton B192

After the International Federation had decided to freeze the development of engines for five years in 2008, the 2.4-litre V8 was only considered as an accessory of the car. Once upon a time, it was one of the elements from which to extract performance advantages, but now FIA has imposed such restrictions – 90° architecture, a 90 kg minimum weight, a 105 mm distance between the cylinders, a defined centre of gravity – that they have, in effect, stopped the escalation of power. So the engine has become an element at the service of the chassis designers and, above all, the teams' aerodynamics.

Over the years, the life of the units has been gradually lengthened by regulation decisions, making the search for reliability ever more difficult. In 2010, each driver was only allowed to have eight engines available to him for the entire season. In substance, the lifespan of an engine was an average of three GPs – including practice, qualifying and racing – and there was free use of them, but on one condition: an engine installed during practice was not allowed to compete in that weekend's grand prix, except in the first race of the season. So it was a bit of a brain teaser: each constructor developed different engine rotation strategies, and all of them did a good job because none were penalised the 10 positions on the starting grid for having fitted a ninth unit.

The engine manufacturers involved in the 2010 championship were Ferrari, Mercedes-Benz and Renault plus one client, Cosworth. To make their lives even more complicated, there was a change in the sporting regulations that prohibited refuelling during pit stops. Until 2009, with short race runs, only a small quantity of fuel was pumped into the cars, so it was possible to "waste" a little more petrol to cool the engine.

But from 2010, fuel consumption became a determining factor in performance. Mercedes had the V8 that consumed least, followed by Renault, while the Ferrari and Cosworth units used a few more litres.

The teams soon worked out that taking on less fuel produced two positive effects. Firstly, the tank could be less capacious, meaning a smaller frontal section of the car, a shorter wheelbase for better aerodynamic efficiency or an optimum balance. Secondly, the less weight that was loaded aboard for the start of a GP – on average in F1 it is estimated that 10 kg equals about 0.3 of a second – gave a performance advantage to cars and drivers. So fuel saving was of maximum importance to all engine developers and their work moved in that direction, each with their own strategies while avoiding any reduction in reliability.

For example Ferrari, who had won the GP of Bahrain on the debut of the F10, were worried and had to replace their engines after practice due to

overheating. There was no breakdown, but the water and oil temperatures of both units had gone out of control due to an error made when evaluating the capacity of the cooling systems. The problem repeated itself again afterwards, causing a crisis in the thermal-plastic materials of the cars' pneumatic valve return systems, which function with 50 bar of compressed air. The result was engine failure due to the breakdown of a piston's pin.

So the men from Maranello asked FIA if they could review the design of the cylinder head, not to improve performance but to return it to reliability: after approval was given and the work was carried out, the problem never occurred again. Solutions that were also useful at Sauber, a Ferrari engine client, who had a few problems with the fuel feed system and they were soon resolved as was the one of cooling when a radiator tubes had broken.

In fact the Ferrari V8, which was certainly the thirstiest in F1, began a development period to reduce fuel consumption without diminishing performance. The results were more than encouraging, because Luca Marmorini's men were able to cut racing consumption by almost 15%, which enabled Fernando Alonso to chase the Vettel and Webber Red Bull Racing cars in the second half of the season. And research did not stop at that point.

The Circus's technicians, increasingly the masters of simulation programmes, elaborated studies aimed at taking certain concepts to the extreme. The 2010 cars were designed

to take on the amount of fuel essential to covering an entire GP's distance, but they soon saw that it was not necessary to fill up to race and win. Due to complicated algorithm mathematics, they developed complex race strategies that enabled some drivers to start with about 15 kg less fuel than the tank could carry. They had immediately worked out that less initial weight could be worth up to half a second a lap in the first part of a GP. And not only that: the Bridgestone tyres would be subjected to less stress, so there could be longer race stints on the condition that fuel was saved in some phases of the race. The mathematical analyses showed it was possible to optimise the time to cover a GP's distance without always using the engine at maximum power.

Meanwhile, the F1 circuits often have sections in which the engine must bring out its torque characteristic rather than its sheer power. In fact, mapping the electronic management systems was programmed to extract the maximum yield from the V8 in the medium power phase, so between 15,500 and 17,000 rpm, which is the range most often used.

And it is due to increasingly sophisticated electronics that it gradually became possible to thin the fuel mix, reducing the quantity of indispensible petrol, so diminishing the amount in the tank at the start.

In 2010, not one driver had to stop at the side of the track having run out of fuel in the final

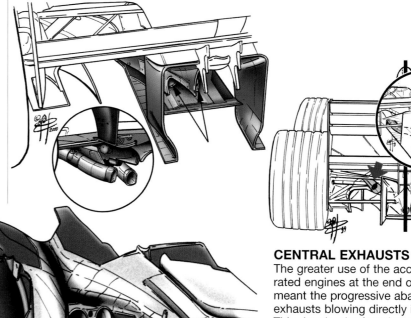

CENTRAL EXHAUSTS

The greater use of the accelerator with aspirated engines at the end of the Eighties meant the progressive abandonment of exhausts blowing directly into the diffuser. This despite the fact that a number of teams continued to test the technique in the early 2000s, among them Williams and McLaren. Downforce became too sensitive to the engine's blow variations between acceleration and deceleration.

stages of the race, which often happened during the period of the Formula consumption of the Eighties' turbo engines.

So that showed the strategy worked marvellously well, but not without some risk.

The "radio controlled" drivers had to manipulate the steering wheel computer to set the various mappings of the engine (the MES electronic management system, the only one to provide five of them) and modify the carburetion, while knowing full well that thinning the mix would produce a slight increase in lap times. An engine specialist in the telemetry van had the task of developing the consumption plan, which had to dovetail with race strategy needs in real time.

We saw on television the cryptic messages from the pits that told the driver how to vary his mapping. Considering the stoichiometric rapport of a thermal engine, in other words the amount of air (comburent) and combustible (petrol) that makes up the mix, they lost three hundredths of a second per lap in certain phases of the race, depending on the Lambda values 0.94 and up to a tenth of a second with Lambda 0.84.

At those times, an increase in the engine's functional temperature – designed to withstand water at 125° and oil at 160° in on the limit conditions – is inevitable.

Taking into account that every engine had to last for about three GPs, it is easy to understand why the effort was made to maintain the life of the power unit and also its efficiency. In the past, a perceptible drop in power was recorded between the first and third race, while with the best 2010 engines, like the Mercedes-Benz, the fall-off was limited to about 30 hp out of the 750 hp available.

Despite the FIA regulation restrictions freezing power units' development, teams were still able to increase their output, essentially operating on the reduction of friction.

A demanding task that involved the lubricant suppliers, who were always able to produce less viscose synthesis oils, but still able to give up to 15 hp a year. Another 5 hp was obtained from the development of petrol.

So the Mercedes engine was credited with over 750 hp and the Ferrari V8 was not far behind, while the world championship-winning Red Bull Racing's Renault lost 15 hp, something less than Cosworth at around 730 hp. One of the most important aspects of the 2010 engine season was the development of the exhausts, which were unaffected by the regulation freeze and which were subjected to continuous updates by the top teams during the season.

The ingenious Adrian Newey, the RB6 designer, knew that to best feed the double diffuser permitted by the tech regs it was necessary to increase the amount of air to the lower part of the car. The Briton was able to channel the exhaust gas to produce a perceptible increase in his cars' aerodynamic load.

A technique that was not immediately understood by his adversaries, but which all of them soon adopted, some channelling the gas above the diffuser, some below it.

The first attempt was less effective, but it made the car more stable to drive because when decelerating the Red Bull drivers complained about the sudden loss of load when the gas stopped blowing.

So Newey asked the Renault engine specialists to make the French unit also blow hot gas when it was not under power. Working on the delay of the advance and a special mapping of the electronic management system, which keeps the butterflies open with fuel feed (they also stopped the spark plugs sparking, keeping only one or two active) the men from Viry Chatillon were able to accommodate the brilliant Adrian. In fact, the combustion phase did not take place in the chamber, avoiding the need to freely provide power for the drive shaft, but in the first half of the hot exhaust: in substance, a post-burning effect was created as with aircraft, which severely tested the reliability of the system.

Sebastian Vettel and Mark Webber were able to exploit this opportunity, especially in qualifying and in certain race conditions.

So the engine was subjected to aerodynamic needs. Suspicions were aroused by the change in the Renault's engine note from a certain point onwards during the season, sparking off the inevitable rumours of presumed irregularity.

Newey had opened a new seam of research that seriously conditioned the design of engines for the 2011 cars. This year's F1 cars are noted precisely for their exploitation of exhaust gas in their diffusers, creating a sort of thermal mini-skirt that reproduces the effects of the wing cars.

Franco Nugnes

THE 1998 FERRARI F300

Another important stage in the integration of the exhausts with the car's aerodynamics happened in 1998, when the Federation ruled that the exhausts were an integral part of a car's body. That rule is still in force and is the basis of a major development carried out in this sector, despite the technical freeze on the improvement of engines in recent years. At the 1999 Grand Prix of Spain, Rory Byrne's Ferrari had high exhausts, which were generalised until the previous season.

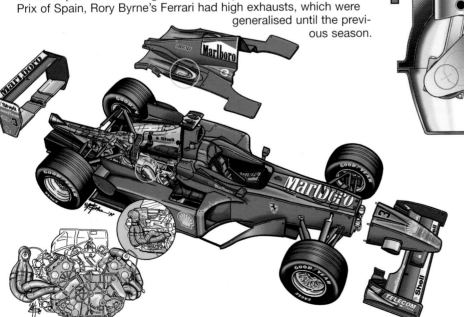

DECELERATION BLOW

The British call it 'hot blowing' and it is a system whereby the exhausts blow into the rear diffuser, even when the engine is decelerating.

The idea was developed by Adrian Newey and it was passed on to Renault's engine specialists to increase a car's aerodynamic load and avoid the sudden instability caused by the closure of the butterflies in deceleration. According to rumour, the valve timing and spark advance are modified, the ignition of the spark plug is inhibited and the amount of petrol is reduced.

In that way, the fuel becomes much leaner in carburetion: the action must not be continuous, otherwise there would be a risk of reduced reliability of the power unit and an increase in fuel consumption.

The 2010 season was the last of Bridgestone's exclusive tyre supply to Formula 1 and it was a year in which the tyres were substantially modified in parallel with, and as a consequence of, the new technical regulations.

Minimum weight of the car, including driver, went from 605 to 620 kg and the increase was brought in together with the abolition of re-fuelling. So the cars' wheelbase was increased to accommodate bigger capacity fuel tanks, with the consequent variation in the static distribution of weight on the axles. In race start condition, the cars weighed at least 100÷120 kg more than in previous season, and this brought a change in the construction of F1 tyres, which now had to withstand not only this extra static weight, but also greater dynamic loads.

Most of the work was carried out on the fronts; as well as modifying the tyres' structure, the dimensions of the profile was reduced by 25 mm from 270/55-13 to 245/55-13 with a consequent diminution of the footprint and, therefore, adhesion.

It should be pointed out, naturally, that the tyre's flexibility meant its footprint changed considerably in relation to speed and, therefore, the loads applied to it. In a static condition, the contact patch with the ground was as big as a postcard, but at 300 kph deformation due to the aerodynamic load generated by the car turned the patch dimensions into that of a piece of A4 paper.

The reduction in profile dimensions was caused by the need to find a better balance of the car, the front tyres of 2009 having had a much higher potential in relation to the rears. That determines a notable responsiveness in changes of direction and high speed cornering, leading to a certain imbalance between the two axles. That penalises the car's performance, causing a loss of grip and a prematurely high wear rate of the rears' treads.

After modifications to the dimensions and construction of the fronts, changes were also made to the build of the rears, with the aim of increasing their mileage capability.

The tyres' typology and compound composition were also changed to lengthen the race segments and to also reduce the time tyres require to reach their optimum operating temperature.

Other important new regulations concerned the number of tyre sets available during race weekend. That went from the 14 of 2009 to the 11 of 2010, six of which were "prime" compound and 5 "option" compound.

For Qualifying and Race the teams still had three "primes" and three "options", but had to start the race with the same set on which each car's qualifying time was set.

Management of pressures when the tyres were cold became more delicate and complicated, especially of those to be used in the race.

The optimum operating pressure for both fronts and rears was usually around 1.3-1.4 bar, values that enabled the tyres to give their best performance in terms of longitudinal grip

FRONT TYRE DIMENSIONS

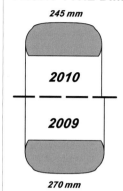

For the 2010 season, the Federation imposed limitations on the width of the front tyres, taking them from 270 mm down to 245 mm, producing a smaller footprint and less adhesion. That forced the teams to seek out a new optimal weight distribution and brakes balance.

and reaction to lateral stress, as well as a uniform and progressive wear rate.

When a car has little fuel on board – like in qualifying – there are few timed laps to run and stress is extremely high, for which reason tyres are needed that quickly reach their optimum operating temperature and pressures to obtain maximum yield.

But things change a lot in a race.

At the start, the car is at maximum weight and the tyres have low temperatures and pressures, having only run the warm-up lap at low speed. Performance and lap times at the beginning of a race are inferior and the driver

	McLaren		Mercedes		Red Bull		Ferrari		Williams		Renault	
	Button	Hamilton	Schumacher	Rosberg	Vettel	Webber	Massa	Alonso	Barrichello	Hulkenberg	Kubica	Petro
Stint	1 2 3	1 2 3 4 5	1 2 3 4 5	1 2 3 4	1 2 3 4 5	1 2 3 4 5	1 2 3 4 5	1 2 3 4 5 6	1 2 3 4 5	1 2 3 4 5 6 7	1 2 3 4	1 2 3
Bahrain	O P	O P	O P	O P	O P	O P	O P	O P	P O	O P O	O P	P
Australia	I O P	I O O	I I O O	I O O	I O	I O O O	I O	I O	I O O	I	I O	I P
Malaysia	O P	P O	O	O P	O P	O P	P O	P O	O P P	O P	O P	O P
China	O I I	O I P I I	O I O I I	O I I	O I P I I	O I P I I	O I O I I	O I I O I I	O I P I I	O I P I P I I	O I I	O I I
Spain	O P	O P	O P	O P O	O P O	O P	O P	O P	O P	O P P	O P	O P
Monaco	O	O P	O P	O P	O P	O P	O P	O P	O P	O	O P	O P P
Turkey	O P	O P	O P	O P	O P	O P P	O P	O P	O P	P O P	O P	O P O
Canada	O P P O P P	P P P O	O P P	P O P	P P O	O P P P O O P P	O P P	O P P P	P P P P O	P P P O P P P		
Europe	O P	O P	P O P O	O P	O P	O P	O P	O P	O P	O P	O P	O P
Great Britain	O P	O P	O P	O P	O P	O P	O P P	O P O	O P	O P	O P	O P P
Germany	O P	O P	O P	O P	O P	O P	O P	O P	O P	O P	O P	O P
Hungary	O P	O P	O P	O	O P	O P	O P	O P	P O	O P	O	O P
Belgium	O	O P I	P I	P I	O P O W W	O P I	O P I	O I P I	P	O P W	O P I	O P I
Italy	O P ·	O	O P	O P	O P	O P	O P	O P	O P	O P	O P	P O
Singapore	O P	O P	O P O	O P	O P	O P	O P	O P	O P	O P	O P	O P
Japan	P O	O P	O P	O P	O P	O P	P	O P	O P	O	O	O
Korea	W W I	W W I	W W I	W W	W W I	W W	W W I	W W I	W W I	W W I I	W W I	W W I
Brasil	O P O	O P P	O P	O P P P O	O P	O P	O P P O	O P	O P O O	O P	O P	O P O
Abu Dhabi	O P	O P	O	O P	O P	O P	O P	O P	O P	P O	P O	O P

P: prime **O**: option (super soft / soft / medium / hard) **I**: intermediate **W**: wet

Talking about TYRES and BRAKES

THERMAL COVERS INSIDE THE WHEEL

The Federation initially decided to abolish thermal covers for 2010, a decision that was rescinded for obvious safety reasons. But they did prohibit systems for heating the inside of the wheels, first used in 1996 by McLaren and Sauber and then adopted by all the major teams.

must use his tyres without deteriorating them to reach minimum threshold of temperature and pressure necessary to guarantee optimum grip.

Pressure too low at the start influence the stiffness and, therefore, the tyres' deformation, so even their structure could deteriorate prematurely. Too high starting pressures could reach operating values over the range should have, reducing footprint areas and, therefore, causing specific pressure on the tyre too high. And all of that would result in their sudden deterioration after just a few laps, with a loss of grip and the need to

change earlier the tyres.

The driver's style at the wheel is decisive under these circumstances.

Too much aggression and nervousness in the early stages of a race, with a full tank and tyres not yet in optimum operating temperatures, could have an effect on their performance and wear rate, with premature degradation and an higher wear rate compared to their potential.

Tyres for the subsequent segments of a race have to support less weight but also sustain greater stress, given the increase in performance; so in this case, too, a precise choice

of cold pressures and the temperature of the heaters must be made in order to ensure their functionality and stability during their use.

In 2010, with same fuel load and compound, performance but principally wear rates not comparable occurred, due to the gentle driving style, very fluid and not aggressive, but still so effective that even led to victory. That was the case, for example, with Jenson Button. After starting on intermediate tyres due to earlier rain in the Grand Prix of Australia, he covered the next 52 laps with slick tyres and soft compound, right through to victory, partly because the asphalt temperature was not especially high.

Naturally, tyres' performance and their wear rate are linked to the type of asphalt, its abrasiveness and surface temperature as well as the stress induced by the type of circuit. Tracks like Barcelona, Istanbul and Suzuka have a high level of lateral stress close to 4.5 g, which lasts for a number of seconds in long corners. They also demand severe braking of over 5 g in deceleration, are harsh and stressful on the tyres.

The choice between Soft and Hard compounds, made partly depending on the temperature of the asphalt, tyres with same structure, ensures an adequate wear rate. On circuits that are not so demanding from the stress point of view and have less grip, like Monaco, Valencia, Montreal and

Force India										Toro Rosso													Lotus									Hispania										Sauber										Virgin									
Sutil				Liuzzi					Buemi					Alguersuari							Trulli					Kovalainen				Chandok/Senna					Senna/Sakon/Klien					De la Rosa /Heidfeld					Kobayashi			Glock					Di Grassi			
2	3	4	5	1	2	3	4	5	1	2	3	4	5	1	2	3	4	5	6	7	1	2	3	4	5	1	2	3	4	1	2	3	4	5	1	2	3	4	5	1	2	3	4	5	1	2	3	1	2	3	4	5	1	2	3	4
O				P	O				P	O				P	O	P					P	O				P	O			O					O	O				O	P				P			P					P			
				I	O				I					I	O	O										I	O			I	P	O			I					I	O				I			I	O				I	O	O	
P				O					O	O	P			P	O						O	P				O	P	P		O	P				O	P										O				O				O	P			
I	O	I	I	O					O					O	I	O	I	I	I	I	O	I	O	I	I	O	I	I		O	I	P	I	I	O	I	P	I	I	O						O				I							I	
P				O	P				O	P	P	P		O	P	P					O	P								O	P				O					O	P				O				O	P				P	O			
P				O	P				P	O	O			P	O	O					O	P				O	P			O	P				O	P				O					O	P			O	P				O	P			
P				O	P				O	P				O	P						P					O				P	O				O	P				O					O	P			P	O				O	P			
P	P			O	P	P			P	P	P	O		O	P	P	P				O	P	P	P	P	P	P	P	O	P	P	O			P					P	P	P			O			P	P	P	O	O	P	P	P	P	O
P				O	P				O	P				O	P						P	O	P			P				O	P				P	O	P			O	P				P	O			P	O	O			P	O			
O				P	O				O	P				P	O						O	P				O	P			O	P				O	P				O	P	P			O	P			O	P				O	P			
P	P	O		P	O	P	O		P					P	O	O					P	O				O	P			O	P				O	P	P			O	P				P	O	P		O	P				P	O			
				P	O				P	O				P							O	P				O	P			O	P				O	P				P	O				O	P			O	P				O	P			
P	I			O	P	P	I	W	O	I	O	I	W	O	I	O	I				O	I				O	I	O	I	O	I	P			O	O	W			O	I	O	I	W	O	P	I	P	W	O	W		O	I			
P	O			O	P				O	P				P	O						O	P				O	P			O					O	P				O	P				P				O	P				O	P			
P				P					O	P	P	O		O	P						O	P	P	O		O	P	P		O	P				O	P				P	O	P			O				P	O				O	P	P		
P				P					P	O				O	P	O					O	P				O	P			O	P				O	P				O	P				P	O			P	O	P							
W	I			W	W	I			W	W	I			W	W	I					W	W	I	I		W	W	I	I	W	W	W	I		W	W	W	W	I	W	W	I	N		W	W	I	W	W				W	W	I		
O				O	P				O	P				O	P						O	P				O	P			O	P				O	P	O			O	P	O			P	O			O	P				O	P	P	O	
O				P					P	O				O	P						P	O				P	O			O	P				O	P				O	P				O	P			O	P	P	O			O	P			

1   **2**   **3**   **4**

Singapore, Bridgestone preferred to use Supersoft and Medium compound. Generally, those city circuits become progressively covered in rubber, so that on race day the conditions are such that they lengthen the duration of the stints. Montreal showed how unpredictable was the race having compound behaviour very different from car to car. It was variable in the different phases, also in relation to the asphalt's temperature, which gradually increased.

The first three on the 2010 Canadian podium, Hamilton, Button and Alonso, used the same strategy of Supersoft-Medium-Medium. They ran the first phase of the race, with full tank, on Supersoft, but it was an extremely short stint that lasted 6-7 laps, as was the second of only 20 laps on the Medium.

The last part of Hamilton's race was particularly surprising, because he covered 44 laps on one set of Medium, confirmation of the evident improvement of the track.

But partly due to the limited adaptation of their cars to the track conditions and compounds the grand prix was a trial for some drivers, with three tyre changes, highs and lows and unpredictable performance.

Due to that experience and Bridgestone's decision to leave Formula 1, there was much more stable and predictable tyre performance in subsequent races, with wider differences between the non-consecutive compounds and, therefore, a lower wear rate.

The 43 laps out of a total of 70 covered by Hungarian GP winner Webber on the Supersoft compound – even though he was aided by the extremely well balanced Red Bull car – confirm the suitability of Bridgestone's change in strategy of supplying longer lasting tyres, even though there was a slight detriment in top performance.

The medium compound performance at Singapore is worth mentioning. Webber was able to run 58 of the 61 laps and finish third despite a contact with Hamilton.

And Vettel's 25 laps on Supersofts to win the Grand Prix of Brazil was in the same league.

But there was nothing new about the rain tyres.

The only grand prix in which they were used – with the start behind the safety car – was on the new Korean track, which did not drain the water well and was especially slippery.

WILLIAMS AIR INTAKES

Their air intakes became ever more aerodynamic devices with the task of cooling delegated to the 'eared' units that protruded from the drums. At the front end, the various winglets had the purpose of cleaning and better directing the air flow towards the central part of the car. At the rear, their job was to create downforce. The sequence shows the evolution of the Williams' air intakes at the rear.

FORCE INDIA

Curious and debateable was Force India's choice of placing their brake calipers so that they overhung the front area of the disc. None of the other teams adopted this solution in 2010, in part because it must have created greater cooling difficulties.

HORIZONTAL CALIPERS

La Red Bull (e la Toro Rosso) sono state le sole squadre di primo piano a conservare le prese coricate in basso all'avantreno anche se la cosa ha comportato diversi problemi di affidabilità (soprattutto a Vettel) legati anche a nuove soluzioni di accoppiamento disco-flangia. Al Gran Premio del Giappone è stato fatto un esperimento portato anche in gara, con le prese in posizione classica verticale. Dal successivo Gran Premio di Corea le pinze sono tornate in posizione coricata.

RENAULT

At the Grand Prix of Canada, Kubica tested Brembo calipers in place of the usual A+P, and at the next race the replacement became permanent on both the French cars.

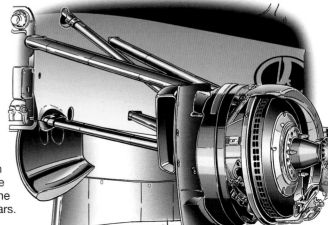

The Federation's abolition of refuelling resulting in the management of the fully loaded cars at the start of every Grand Prix, and a weight increase to 620 kg obviously conditioned the development of 2010 braking systems.

If one considers that the energy to be dissipated under braking is no less than the jump in the car's kinetic energy ($Ec=1/2 \cdot m \cdot \Delta v^2$), one can reasonably understand how an increase in mass translates into a proportional rise in stress on the braking system equal to the speed of the vehicle.

It was first thought that the speed would be reduced due to the mass increase having a negative effect on acceleration out of a corner, but instead it often increased its value following the introduction of the F-duct or blown wing: that cut resistance to advancement on the straights.

Another fundamental element that conditioned the cars' design and use of the 2010 systems was the front tyre section reduction.

This stratagem allowed a more homogeneous distribution of grip and braking power on the ground by the two axles, controlling the effect of the increased

PISTONS

For the 2010 season, Red Bull dropped its unique calipers with four pistons at the rear used in 2009 and moved on to the classic six piston system, like all the other teams.

weight and contributing to not aggravating the dimensions of the front braking system too much, dimensions which, anyway, are partially limited by the regulations.

On that note, it is worth remembering that the regulation does not permit the use of brake discs of more than a 278 mm diameter and a maximum thickness of 28 mm.

The above led to a 5%-10% increase in energy exerted on the front axle and 35%-40% on the rear, compared to the 2009 season when, it will be recalled, the braking action was greatly unbalanced at the front.

It also produced a braking balance that was better distributed between both axles, which was around 54%-56% instead of 2009's 60%-62%.

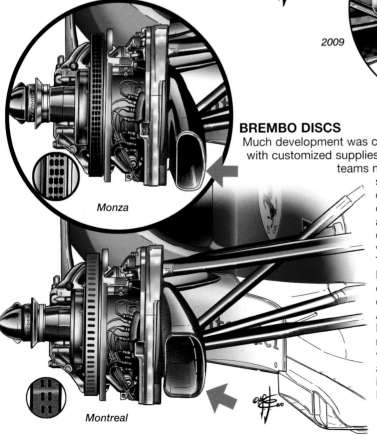

2009

Monza

Montreal

BREMBO DISCS

Much development was carried out on brake discs, with customized supplies according to the various teams needs. As well as the squads in the list of caliper suppliers, Brembo often provided McLaren and Force India with its discs even if equipped with various calipers.

The illustration shows the Montreal and Monza discs, with holes made exclusively for Ferrari. A cure also applied to Red Bull and Sauber, with the red arrow indicating the various dimensions of the air intakes, which were increased for the Grand Prix of Canada.

The perceptible increase in braking energy at the rear end also benefitted from the decision to abolish KERS, the device that subtracted part of the braking torque to recharge the batteries that powered the electric motor/alternator.

The new braking system design regulations substantially led to the return of the so-called 'square system' and, therefore, similar calipers front and rear.

Red Bull, which was decidedly extreme in 2009 with a four piston caliper of reduced dimensions at the rear, went back to one caliper with six pistons, similar to the one on the front axle.

And because much of the energy during braking is transformed into heat, the development and aggravation of brake disc ventilation continued.

The number of holes increased, while the diameter contracted with the objective of maximising the surface in contact between the carbon fibre and the air. In some cases the holes themselves were oriented in line with the direction of wheel rotation to support the fluid motor and differentiate in that way between the right and left discs.

The decisive increase in stress under braking also aggravated the longitudinal and lateral loads to which all the elements of the corner are subjected during deceleration and going into a curve, and this created quite a number of problems for those who underestimated this aspect, especially considering the ban imposed this season on Metal Matrix material for the production of the uprights in favour of a more standard and less rigid aluminium. Those loads, which involve the disc and bell – the drag element of the disc – connected to the hub and brake caliper fixed to the upright, are amplified in case the latter is positioned under the axle, as in the case of the Red Bull. It is not by chance that, in order to verify alternative solutions to the one used at the beginning of the season, the Milton Keynes team tested briefly the installation of the caliper in a vertical position at Monza, as on the Ferrari and McLaren.

This solution was only raced at the GP of Japan, before returning to the prone position for the season's subsequent three races.

3

2

2010 BRAKE CALIPER SUPPLIERS
BREMBO: Ferrari, Red Bull, Mercedes, Sauber, Toro Rosso, Renault (from the Grand Prix of Europe), HRT
A+P: Williams, Force India, Virgin.
AKEBONO: McLaren

There were not many new features in this area, apart from the addition of the F-duct control by most teams that adopted this development for the 2010 season. But that did not include Ferrari or Mercedes-Benz; their systems were operated by the driver's left foot.

The most interesting change took place at Ferrari, whose driver Fernando Alonso requested a simpler steering wheel, with a number of functions similar to those he had on his Renault. The frame of the F10's wheel was identical, as can be seen in the comparison with Felipe Massa's F60 unit, but two paddles and some buttons had disappeared. In their place came a large central paddle similar to that of the Renault, as can be seen in the illustration of the French car's steering wheel, but Ferrari's became even bigger and ran more functions. The wheel of the star car, Red Bull, was also unchanged, as were those of the season's other key teams.

But there were new features on the McLaren, with the lower part of the wheel cut at the specific request of the drivers.

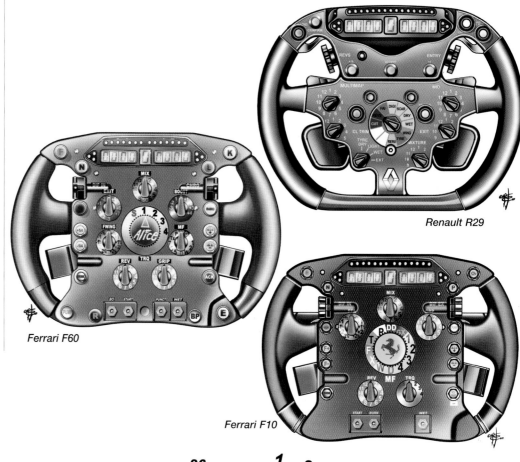

Renault R29

Ferrari F60

Ferrari F10

ALONSO'S STEERING WHEEL

1	*LEDs that show when to change gear.*
2	*Shows the gear currently engaged.*
3	*Pit lane speed limiter.*
4	*Over-rev.*
5	*Differential exit control.*
6	*Different set up of the throttle pedal.*
7	*Auxiliary oil pump.*
8-9	*Allows the change of functions after having selected the programme with the central control.*
10	*Confirms the selection has been carried out.*
11	*Multi-function switch to change programmes.*
12	*Different torque based on the tyres fitted.*
13	*Engine map.*
14	*Allows tyre warm-up by zigzagging during the pre-race lap.*
15	*Management of starting parameters.*
16	*Management of the various engine revs.*
17	*Water bottle.*
18-19	*Rise and fall settings.*
20	*Front flap adjustment settings.*
21	*Radio.*
22	*Differential when entering a corner.*
23	*Neutral.*
24	*Operates the flap after pre-setting.*
25	*Reproduces the FIA marshals' flags.*
26	*Fuel mixture.*

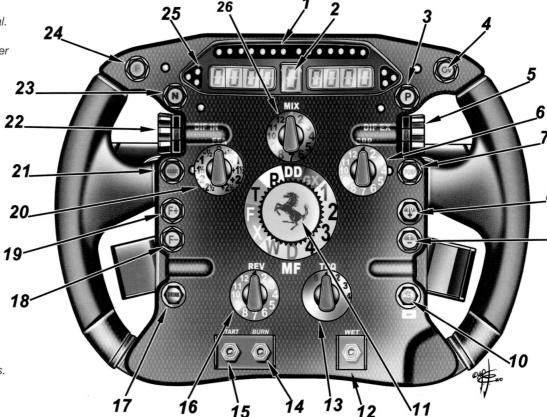

REAR OF THE FERRARI STEERING WHEEL

The wheel was completely unchanged at the back, with just four paddles and a single rocker arm for the management of the gears, so that the driver could change up or down with one hand if the other was doing something else.

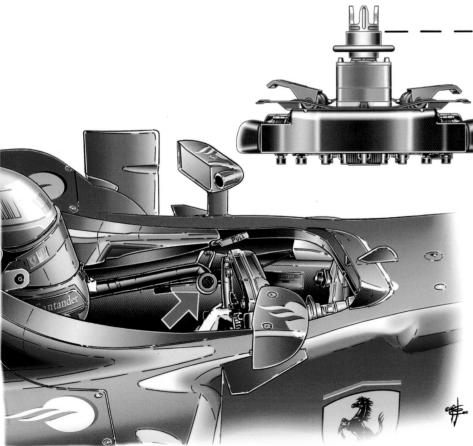

F-DUCT CONTROL

The different driving position revealed by the longer bell housing applied behind Alonso's steering wheel created greater difficulty for Massa when operating the F-duct control, at least in the position introduced in Turkey. The Brazilian, who drives with his arms slightly less drawn up, found that his left hand was too far forward in relation to the "hole" that had to be blocked off, so he had to take his hand completely off the wheel to operate the duct. Ferrari resolved the problem by moving the hole to a location near the footrest so that both drivers could operate it with their left foot.

2008

McLAREN STEERING WHEEL

After having been unchanged for many years, the McLaren steering wheel has been subjected to a continuous evolution in recent years. In 2010 the display was integrated after having previously been separated from the steering wheel and fixed immediately above the dashboard.

During the same season, Hamilton asked for the lower part to be cut for easier manipulation. The switch positions were also slightly modified, there being fewer of them than on the Ferrari but in that sense it should be remembered that in 2009 McLaren introduced six paddles to the back of the wheel and they remained in 2010.

2009

2010

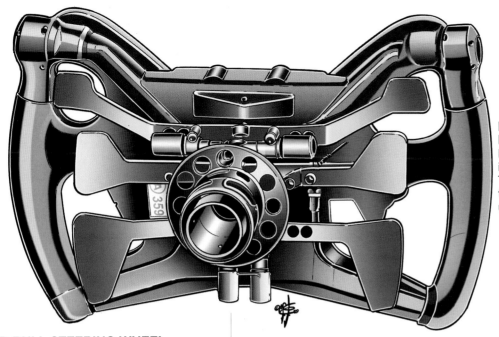

RED BULL:
REAR OF STEERING WHEEL

Red Bull also used six paddles at the rear of its wheel, which was made of titanium.
The two upper levers control the differential, those in the centre the gearbox and the lower units the clutch.

RED BULL STEERING WHEEL

Red Bull and Toro Rosso are the only teams not to have integrated their displays into the steering wheel, which remained the same horizontal X shape once also used by McLaren. The buttons are many and also on the spokes.
In detail, they are:

1 Different positions for the control of the differential when entering (left) and exiting (right) corners, activated by the couple of added paddles above (**6-22**).

2 Pit lane speed limiter (**3-4-24**); with the FAIL button selected sensors are disconnected (**3** and **24**).

5 Confirms reception of radio messages.

7 Activates the front wing's flap adjustor after having selected the incidence variation with the paddle (**11**).

8 Changes the display functions.

9 Reverse gear with protection.

10 Free button.

12 Engine map.

13 Clutch setting.

14 Regulates the air/fuel mixture in relation to track and weather conditions.

15 Setting to use, dependent on the type of tyres fitted.

16 Double paddle for the clutch.

17 Drink button.

18 Activation of brake balance after adjustment made using a paddle on the left of the cockpit.

20 Button to activate tyre warmer.

21 Brings in the oil pump.

23 Inserts neutral.

25 Radio.

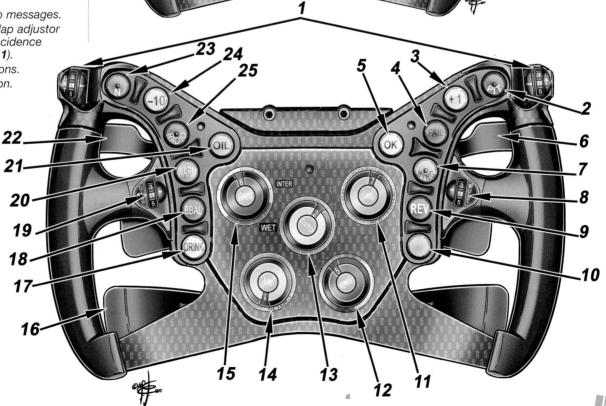

The reduction in front tyre dimensions and technical regulation modifications caused variations in the design, geometry and rigidity of the cars' suspensions.

Cars' minimum weight was increased to 620 kg as a result of refuelling abolition during races, and that meant they would weigh about 100÷120 kg more on the starting grid than the previous year.

This increase of about 20% brought different approaches from the technicians as they defined their suspensions' set-ups.

In 2009 the qualifying set-up, in which cars competed with 40÷60 kg of fuel, was also enough for the first race stint, but it was equally effective for successive segments, which were run with similar fuel loads.

But in 2010, qualifying took place with the minimum possible amount of fuel on board – 15÷20 kg for the laps of the final run – while at the start the cars weighed much more, between 120÷140 kg.

The problem was to find the best compromise in terms of rigidity to the ground, roll stiffness and damping in the two conditions of extreme weight, a compromise that still had to be effective during the whole race as the fuel load diminished.

To this technical problem was added the variation in the dimensions of the front tyres; the reduction in tread width and, therefore, of the tyre's potential influenced the static division of weight.

Compared to 2009, the mass was moved towards the front by about 2%, nearing a value of around 48%, to try to make the car's balance as neutral as possible.

Despite these variations in the car's weight, vertical rigidity at the front stayed similar, while roll increased.

Meanwhile, at the rear the rigidity of the torsion bars was increased due to the greater weight of a full fuel tank and that also diminished the risk of the car bottoming as it hit the asphalt; hardly anyone used an anti-roll bar, but the inerter was always present to dampen the oscillation effect and ensure better grip.

From the suspension configuration point of view, the general tendency at the front was to raise the car's nose to leave greater space for air flow directed to the rear end, keel and sidepods.

Consequently, the mounts were moved upwards, but the designers still had to take into account needs in terms of the height of the roll centre, camber recovery and other elements dictated by the new Bridgestone fronts.

Generally, we saw a certain reduction in camber, with average values between 2°75'÷3°25' depending on the circuit, and a slight diminution of recovery during jolting to equal value of anti-dive.

Having said that, the layout used by everyone was push rod; the biggest variations were seen in the position of the drive box, on the

FERRARI

The F10 retained the classic position of the steering arm incorporated into the upper wishbone, despite the arms being raised due to the nose's greater height from the ground.

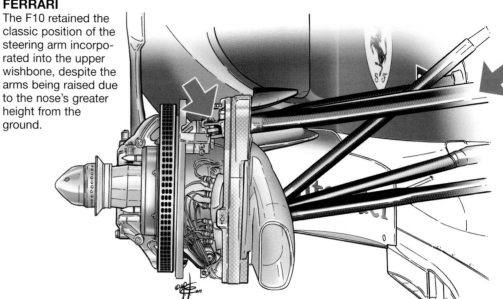

vertical distance between the mounts of the upper and lower wishbones and their inclination, which determined the anti-dive values.

In the case of Ferrari, the mounts were fairly close to each other in the vertical direction, with the steering box and, therefore, the arms incorporated into the upper lever, which was at more or less half the height of the monocoque.

The inclination of the wishbones in the longitudinal direction was not especially noticeable.

The Mercedes-Benz choice was different, with the steering box and arms just a little lower than the upper wishbone, with the lower mounts very low on the monocoque and close together.

While retaining the same disposition and a relatively similar distance, the suspension levers and steering arms of the Red Bull were decidedly more inclined upwards and were fixed on the monocoque in a higher position from the ground; the monocoque and nose were much further from the ground to favour and better direct air flow in the sidepods and to the under the body.

The longitudinal inclination of the wishbones was not especially high.

McLaren's answer was the same: the only difference was the much lower position of the steering box, with relative arms just above the height of the wheel centre.

But we should point out the notable inclination of the upper arm, a sign of particular attention being paid to the suspension's anti-dive values, an inclination present with the same high values on both the Force India and Williams.

It was Williams that came up with a new front suspension development, which had the torsion bars connected to each other by a horizontal element. That enabled them to uncouple the vertical jolting movements from those of roll.

As far as rear suspension is concerned Red Bull and Toro Rosso stood out from the other teams, using and developing the pull rod technique, so with a tie rod link that was also on the 2009 cars.

The position of the brake callipers stayed horizontal and low, conditioning the upright design and the position of the suspension wishbone mounts. The upper lever was very long and almost horizontal, so that it practically joined at car's centreline with the one from the other side in the upper area of the gearbox. The inclination of the lower lever was slight, however.

As with the previous season, the tie rod was much inclined and acted on the pivot block, which was in a very low position and had a sophisticated geometry to work the torsion bars which were also placed in a very low position and, therefore, easily accessible.

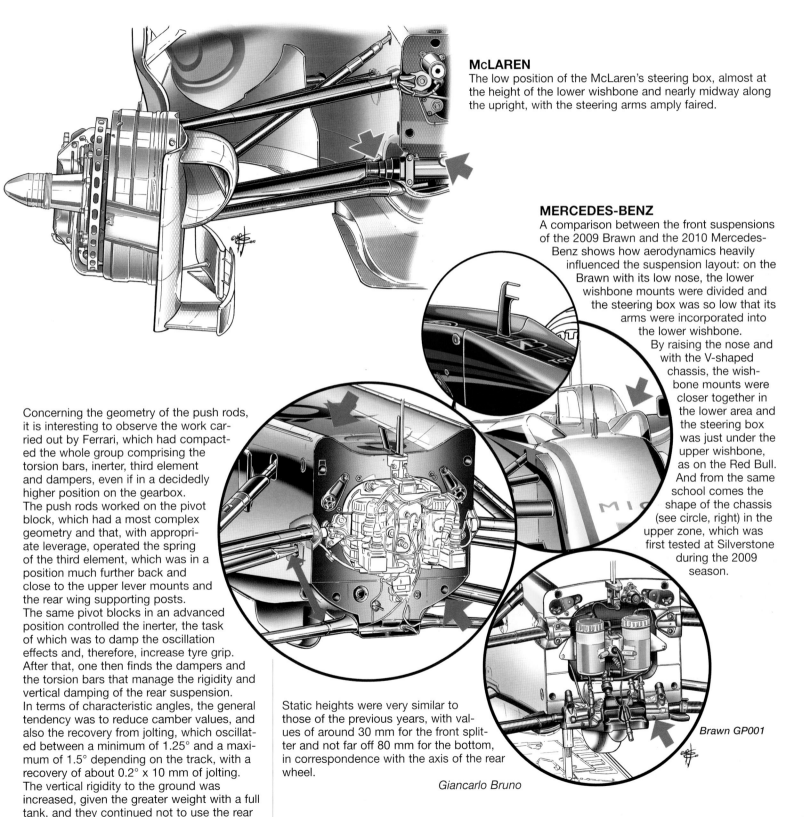

McLAREN
The low position of the McLaren's steering box, almost at the height of the lower wishbone and nearly midway along the upright, with the steering arms amply faired.

MERCEDES-BENZ
A comparison between the front suspensions of the 2009 Brawn and the 2010 Mercedes-Benz shows how aerodynamics heavily influenced the suspension layout: on the Brawn with its low nose, the lower wishbone mounts were divided and the steering box was so low that its arms were incorporated into the lower wishbone.

By raising the nose and with the V-shaped chassis, the wishbone mounts were closer together in the lower area and the steering box was just under the upper wishbone, as on the Red Bull. And from the same school comes the shape of the chassis (see circle, right) in the upper zone, which was first tested at Silverstone during the 2009 season.

Concerning the geometry of the push rods, it is interesting to observe the work carried out by Ferrari, which had compacted the whole group comprising the torsion bars, inerter, third element and dampers, even if in a decidedly higher position on the gearbox.
The push rods worked on the pivot block, which had a most complex geometry and that, with appropriate leverage, operated the spring of the third element, which was in a position much further back and close to the upper lever mounts and the rear wing supporting posts.
The same pivot blocks in an advanced position controlled the inerter, the task of which was to damp the oscillation effects and, therefore, increase tyre grip. After that, one then finds the dampers and the torsion bars that manage the rigidity and vertical damping of the rear suspension.
In terms of characteristic angles, the general tendency was to reduce camber values, and also the recovery from jolting, which oscillated between a minimum of 1.25° and a maximum of 1.5° depending on the track, with a recovery of about 0.2° x 10 mm of jolting. The vertical rigidity to the ground was increased, given the greater weight with a full tank, and they continued not to use the rear anti-roll bars.

Static heights were very similar to those of the previous years, with values of around 30 mm for the front splitter and not far off 80 mm for the bottom, in correspondence with the axis of the rear wheel.

Giancarlo Bruno

Brawn GP001

RED BULL

With the liberalisation of the double diffuser at the end of 2009, observers thought that Red Bull would have dropped the rear pull rod layout, but the RB6 retained it and that enabled the suspension's centre of gravity to be lowered. Also note the completely prone position of the brake callipers for the same reason. On the other hand, the Red Bull layout has always required highly complex modification when new regulations were brought in.

RED BULL

The RB6 retained just about the same position for its steering box, up high with the non-faired arms at about the height of the upper wishbone and the lower units set into almost the centre of the V-chassis.

WILLIAMS

The Williams' front suspension had two peculiarities that distinguished it from many other layouts: one was the position of the steering arm, which was near the suspension's upper wishbone at a height about halfway up the rim, no longer being incorporated into the upper arm, as in 2009.

The second was the connection between the torsion bars. The end of one of the bars was, as usual, inserted into the rocker arm close to the push rod; the other was not fitted to the monocoque, but connected by a small horizontal bar to the other unit. That way, the team achieved the "connection" between the two front suspension set-ups, which worked differently dependent on their movement. There was also a similar layout at the rear end.

WILLIAMS: INERTER

Most teams made use of the inerter which, with its transverse oscillating mass, damped the effects of oscillation and conserved the best adhesion.

The illustration shows the Williams inerter, a device that was easily seen, even during testing.

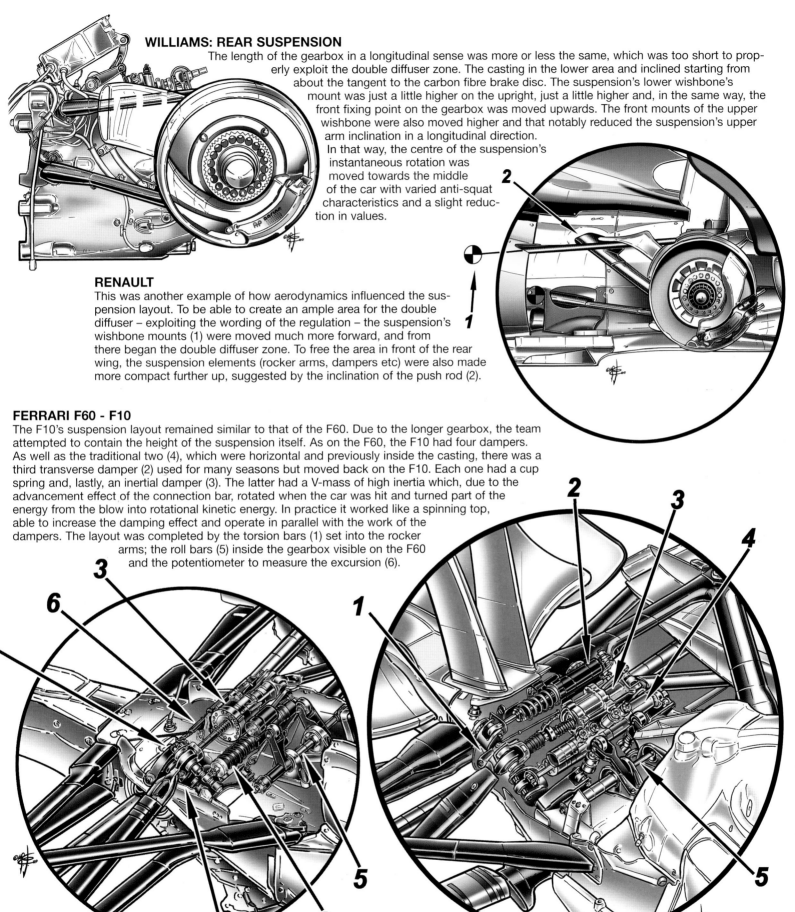

WILLIAMS: REAR SUSPENSION

The length of the gearbox in a longitudinal sense was more or less the same, which was too short to properly exploit the double diffuser zone. The casting in the lower area and inclined starting from about the tangent to the carbon fibre brake disc. The suspension's lower wishbone's mount was just a little higher on the upright, just a little higher and, in the same way, the front fixing point on the gearbox was moved upwards. The front mounts of the upper wishbone were also moved higher and that notably reduced the suspension's upper arm inclination in a longitudinal direction.

In that way, the centre of the suspension's instantaneous rotation was moved towards the middle of the car with varied anti-squat characteristics and a slight reduction in values.

RENAULT

This was another example of how aerodynamics influenced the suspension layout. To be able to create an ample area for the double diffuser – exploiting the wording of the regulation – the suspension's wishbone mounts (1) were moved much more forward, and from there began the double diffuser zone. To free the area in front of the rear wing, the suspension elements (rocker arms, dampers etc) were also made more compact further up, suggested by the inclination of the push rod (2).

FERRARI F60 - F10

The F10's suspension layout remained similar to that of the F60. Due to the longer gearbox, the team attempted to contain the height of the suspension itself. As on the F60, the F10 had four dampers. As well as the traditional two (4), which were horizontal and previously inside the casting, there was a third transverse damper (2) used for many seasons but moved back on the F10. Each one had a cup spring and, lastly, an inertial damper (3). The latter had a V-mass of high inertia which, due to the advancement effect of the connection bar, rotated when the car was hit and turned part of the energy from the blow into rotational kinetic energy. In practice it worked like a spinning top, able to increase the damping effect and operate in parallel with the work of the dampers. The layout was completed by the torsion bars (1) set into the rocker arms; the roll bars (5) inside the gearbox visible on the F60 and the potentiometer to measure the excursion (6).

Ferrari F60

Ferrari F10

The 2010 was a season packed with more new developments than any other in recent years. Even more so than 2009, when the Federation imposed its technical revolution. And the most sensational of them all was McLaren's F-duct.

It was first obstructed by the team's adversaries, who tried to block it by saying it was a mobile aerodynamic device. But once it had been approved, it was copied by all the teams, except the three minors, Lotus, HRT and Virgin.

Originally called the F-flap – the flown flap – by McLaren, the F-duct could even have been used by the team from Woking at the end of the 2009 season, starting from a similar concept but it produced opposing results, in other words the division of the rear wing's trailing edge, introduced by McLaren at the 2008 Monaco GP. At that time, the intake in the main plane exited with a second trailing edge in the spine of the plane itself, dividing the exit and avoiding the separation of the fluid vein and, therefore, increasing efficiency. In practice, the team created the effect of two blown planes in one single section.

In the case of the F-duct, the corner in which the low speed flap blow took place virtually stalled the plane, so reducing its ability to create downforce and, therefore, increasing top speed. McLaren preferred to delay its introduction so as not to give its adversaries time to study the system during the winter break, also because, at the heart of its efficiency was a careful study of the passages of the various channels of air inside the chassis and engine cover. With the Federation's blockage of all modifications to the monocoque by homologation at the start of the year, that would have created a number of difficulties for the teams that wanted to copy the system.

The point contested by the teams at the beginning of the season concerned the management of the system: a variation of downforce by the direct and precise intervention of the driver. There was nothing prohibited about dividing the air flow inside the engine's intake. And every single component of the system was perfectly legal, as was the slot in the rear of the flap, because the regulation that said there was to be no flexing between the flap and principal plane had been respected.

But it is obvious that this system needed precise control to be useful, otherwise the risk was that it would also begin to function in fast corners with consequent problems for the driver. And that is where the front air intake came in, the set-up of which was maniac during winter testing with different shapes at just about every session, measurements with Pitot tubes and various other instruments. This intake worked on the system in such a simple manner that it was almost laughable; it was based on an American Cold War aeronautical patent, and was a sort of air valve that guided the flow in two different directions. It did, in fact, feed a channelling that went through the inside of

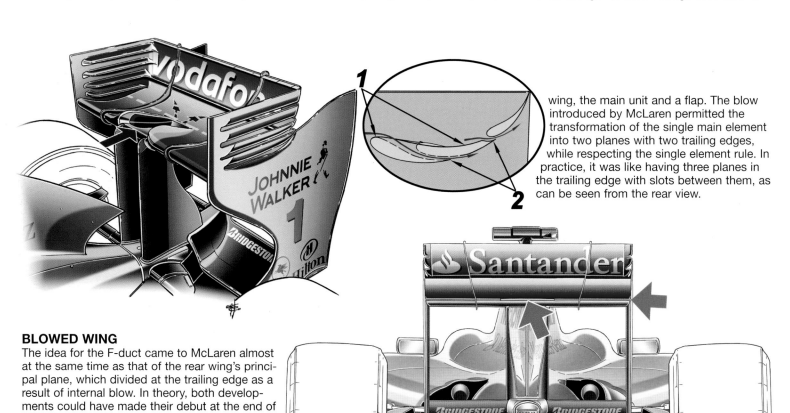

wing, the main unit and a flap. The blow introduced by McLaren permitted the transformation of the single main element into two planes with two trailing edges, while respecting the single element rule. In practice, it was like having three planes in the trailing edge with slots between them, as can be seen from the rear view.

BLOWED WING

The idea for the F-duct came to McLaren almost at the same time as that of the rear wing's principal plane, which divided at the trailing edge as a result of internal blow. In theory, both developments could have made their debut at the end of 2009, because the former was introduced at Monaco that year, but the team preferred to delay them so as not give its adversaries time to come up with a similar system during the winter break. Now let's analyse how the 2009 split main plane worked, one which was copied that same season by Sauber and Williams. The regulation allows a maximum of just two planes for the rear

New DEVELOPMENTS

the cockpit and united the flows that went inside the engine air intake and cover with an X-intersection. But that was not enough. To make everything work, the amount of air flow had to be made intermittent in the X-intersection. It was always thought it was the driver's left knee that operated this change as it interacted with the air flow from the front intake. But McLaren designer Paddy Lowe confirmed that, right from the first race, control was carried out by the pilot's left elbow through a hole in the channelling at his height in the car. In mixed sections of a track and corners the hole was left open to let air into the cockpit but, more importantly, it did not blow into the large fin. The inside flow was then directed down to the level of the lower plane, increasing its efficiency. On the straights, the driver just moved his elbow, blocked the hole and the flow was directed towards the engine air intake, making the air flow change direction

towards the upper part of the wing – just like points switch the direction of railway lines – making it stall as a result of its exit from the rear slot. No mobile device was set in motion, as everything was managed by speed and air pressure inside the channels in the MP4-25's large fin.

While all the other teams copied the McLaren system, with the only variation the position of the entry intake and its control – the driver's left elbow in most cases, but his left foot on the Ferrari and Mercedes-Benz – Williams took a different design direction to the blown rear wing system. The diagrams (p.34) show the single duct arrangement that was used successfully from the Valencia GP onwards. It differs from the conventional McLaren method in which a three-way duct system is used with fluidic switching.

The rear wing flap was connected by a long duct directly to the hole in the driver's seat,

positioned under his left thigh.

The duct formed an airtight seal along its entire path. As the duct had to be fitted after the chassis had been designed, it had to take a non-optimal path to escape the confines of the tight chassis. The duct wrapped around behind the driver's seat and exited out of the chassis, high up behind the headrest area. The inlet to the duct was sealed by the driver's leg resting on top of it.

To stall the rear wing, the driver lifted his leg slightly, breaking the seal to the duct inlet and allowing air to flow from the ambient pressure area of the cockpit into the duct.

This air was then sucked through by the low pressure acting on the rear wing flap suction rearward surface.

Once the driver allowed the air to flow through the duct, it exited from a narrow 1 mm slot that ran the length of the rear wing flap's suction surface. That was sufficient to

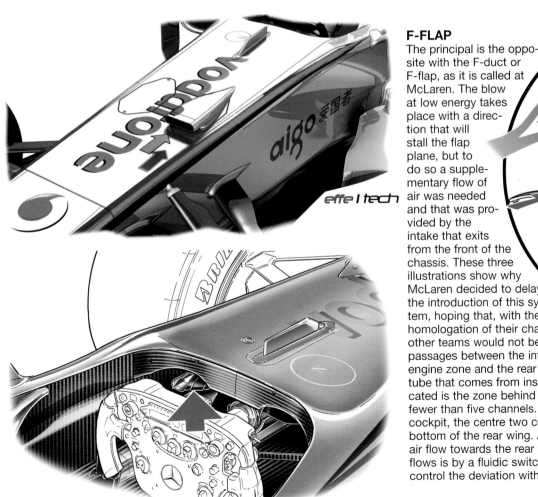

effe I tech

F-FLAP

The principal is the opposite with the F-duct or F-flap, as it is called at McLaren. The blow at low energy takes place with a direction that will stall the flap plane, but to do so a supplementary flow of air was needed and that was provided by the intake that exits from the front of the chassis. These three illustrations show why McLaren decided to delay the introduction of this system, hoping that, with the homologation of their chassis, the other teams would not be able to create the optimum passages between the interior of the monocoque, the engine zone and the rear wing. One can clearly see the section of the tube that comes from inside the front of the chassis and how complicated is the zone behind the roll bar and engine air intake, with no fewer than five channels. The one down low on the left comes from the cockpit, the centre two cool the oil radiator and send a flow of air to the bottom of the rear wing. As well as feeding the engine, its intake direct air flow towards the rear wing flap: management of these various air flows is by a fluidic switch, made from an American Cold War patent to control the deviation without hydraulic elements.

disrupt the flow attached to the flap, causing it to separate from the surface. The separated rear wing lost significant downforce and drag, which was not a problem for the driver as long as he had activated the system when the car was not limited by grip and he was able to use full throttle. Drag reduction was about 7%, which was enough to increase top speed by around 7 kph.

A second new development that set a trend during the 2010 season was exhaust blow into the diffusers, first used by Red Bull. As early as the 2009 season the RB5 exhausts were at the sides of the sidepods terminals, but the RB6 went even further. That car's exhausts were initially positioned even lower but then made to interact with the diffusers' lateral channels. As with the pull rod suspension layout, this Adrian Newey development has its origins in the past. In 1983, to be exact, when Renault brought in exhaust blow into the diffusers at the Grand Prix of Monaco.

Newey's system dominated the whole season and there is complete coverage of it in the Engines chapter, because it required a significant contribution from the power unit specialists to find the special mapping that would ensure greater consistency of hot air flow that had to be "shot" into the diffusers.

Ferrari was one of the teams that best interpreted exhaust blow into the diffusers, successfully introducing low exhausts at the GP of Valencia.

But Mercedes-Benz, for example, had to postpone their system's introduction despite the fact that both Williams and McLaren came up with theirs for Silverstone, but there again even this debut was a Grand Prix late. The problem was the great deal of heat from the exhausts, which had to be blown at over 600°C towards the lateral channels: it literally deformed them.

So the teams turned to a new material called Pyrossic, a mix of ceramics, glass and resin produced by one single factory in Europe with its headquarters in France, the supply of which was staggered, given the unexpectedly substantial demand for their product from all the F1 teams.

The cost of this latest technical sophistication was enough to set heads spinning – about £Stg1 million. Of that £Stg200,000 was spent on making the exhausts, £Stg300,000 testing them so that they could be tuned to the engine's characteristics and £Stg100,000 for the construction of at least five new diffusers. The rest went on wind tunnel testing and CFD system calculations.

After those two major new developments that conditioned the season, Ferrari also stepped into the spotlight with two new features: the angled engine-gearbox group and rims with aerodynamic devices as an integral part of them.

While something really new to modern Formula 1, the inclined engine-gearbox assembly was not unique. Experiments were carried out on just such a feature on the Arrows A2 31 years ago by Tony Southgate, a car driven by Riccardo Patrese and Jochen Mass. In 1979, the inclination was 4° and the car, a concentration of new developments, was uncompetitive. In the case of the Ferrari F10, the inclination was only 3.5°, which

F-FLAP LAYOUT

In this profile view of the McLaren MP4-25 are all the elements that make up the F-flap. They are:
1) the cockpit inlet;
2) the vent into the cockpit;
3) the transfer tube that sends the pneumatic control signal to the engine cover;
4) the roll hoop inlet;
5) the fluidic switch;
6) the slot in the flap;
7) the alternative outlet above the lower rear wing.

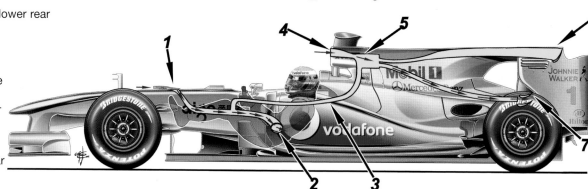

PASSIVE F-FLAP PHASE

A flow of accelerated air enters the front (1) of the chassis and exits inside the chassis (2) without interfering with the air that enters the engine's roll hoop inlet (3) and which, without deviation, goes directly to the lower part of the rear wing (4).

STALLED F-FLAP

The air that goes into the front intake (1), blocked by the driver's elbow closing the cockpit hole (2), rises to the upper part of the channelling (3) and moves on to the chassis to interfere with the control "box" (4), like a points change on a railway line but this one was activated pneumatically. It switches the air flow to the flap in the upper part of the rear wing (5).

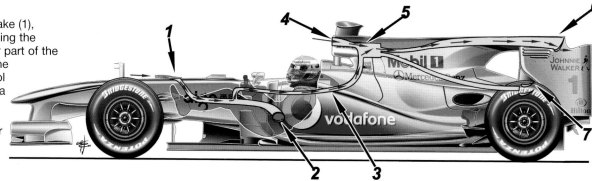

enabled Maranello to raise all of the rear end to produce really advanced aerodynamics. Abandoning the development of the F60 half way through the 2009 season enabled the team to fully concentrate on the new project, making radical technical decisions such as the inclined engine. A technique which, combined with the greater length of the gearbox, meant the team could position the hole that fed the double (it became triple) central diffuser further forward, creating a longer aerodynamic channel that could be exploited.

The F10's rims surprised the opposition as they had been designed to partially recreate the beneficial effect of the lenticular fairing in carbon fibre, which was banned by the Federation for 2010.

When Ferrari introduced this new development, it upset its opponents because it seemed to contravene the spirit of the regulation, which banned aerodynamic devices applied to the rims.

But the solution adopted for the F10 respected the letter of the regulation, because it was an integral part of the rim's design and was fully homologated and approved by FIA. It was also made in materials prescribed by the norm, unlike the rim covers as they were in carbon fibre. The two rings that improved air extraction were made of cast magnesium, like the rim itself.

New from Mercedes-Benz was the knife edge roll bar, which produced a notable reduction of the frontal section, especially when the two new "ear" shaped engine air intakes were introduced at the Grand Prix of Spain; they were very low, so as not to interfere with the flow of air to the rear wing. But this was a development that caused some perplexity on the safety front, because if the car rolled over on a soft surface the knife edge part of the roll bar would sink dangerously into the ground.

WILLIAMS

Once the driver allowed the air to flow through the duct, it would exit along the narrow 1 mm slot along the length of the rear wing flap's suction surface. To maximise drag reduction, the slot had to be located forward of the flap – or indeed the main plane – to stall as much of the wing as possible.

This flow was sufficient to disrupt the air attached to the flap, causing it to separate from the surface.

The separated rear wing lost significant downforce and drag, which was not a problem for the driver as long as he only activated the system when the car is at full throttle. Drag reduction was about 7%, which was enough to increase top speed by 7 kph.

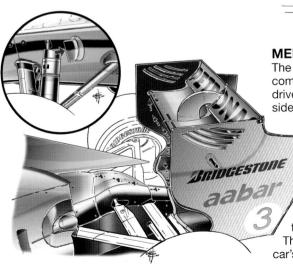

MERCEDES-BENZ

The system devised by Mercedes-Benz was completely different; it was operated by the driver's left foot and fed by intakes at the sides of the cockpit.

There was no direct contact between the engine's roll hoop inlet and the rear wing, because there was no fin, linked to the bib splitter roll bar. Channelling through which to feed the F-duct took a complicated and expensive route inside the diffusers' lateral channels, passing through the interior of the end plates of the wing itself.

That was a choice that compromised the car's development in this sector.

FERRARI

The Ferrari layout was the same, of course, with channelling in the small amount of available space between the chassis, mechanical components and body. Control was by the driver blocking the hole (1) near the footrest (left). Initially, the hole was to the side of the steering wheel (2) as described in the Cockpits chapter. The feed came from two "ear" like intakes (3) at the sides of the roll bar, with the control box at the point of intersection (4) and the channelling that comes from the cockpit. Ferrari used blow into the flap (5) throughout the season, while both McLaren and Red Bull moved on to the more effective blow into the principal plane, first brought out by Force India preceded by Sauber, but the Swiss team dropped the feature immediately.

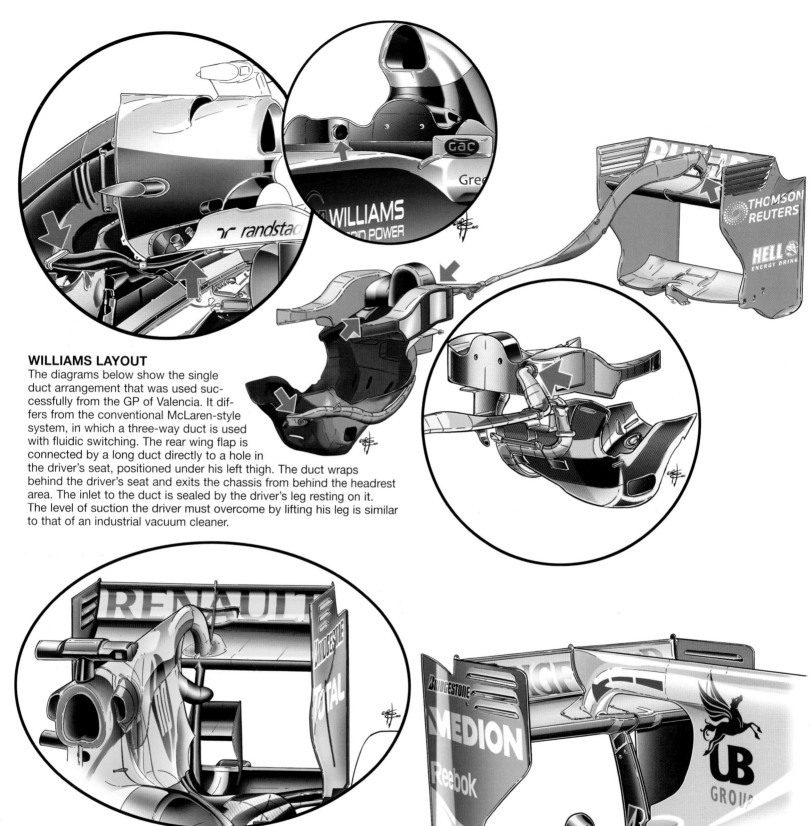

WILLIAMS LAYOUT

The diagrams below show the single duct arrangement that was used successfully from the GP of Valencia. It differs from the conventional McLaren-style system, in which a three-way duct is used with fluidic switching. The rear wing flap is connected by a long duct directly to a hole in the driver's seat, positioned under his left thigh. The duct wraps behind the driver's seat and exits the chassis from behind the headrest area. The inlet to the duct is sealed by the driver's leg resting on it. The level of suction the driver must overcome by lifting his leg is similar to that of an industrial vacuum cleaner.

RENAULT - FORCE INDIA

Renault was the last of the leading teams to adopt the F-duct. It did so at the Grand Prix of Belgium, and became the team that, possibly, achieved the best results with that system. Fernando Alonso learnt to his cost how effective the Renault F-duct was, because he was unable to pass Vitaly Petrov to win the drivers' title in the final GP of the season. The French car's blow went directly into the main plane, as it did when it made its debut on the Force India, which was later copied by Red Bull and McLaren.

New **DEVELOPMENTS**

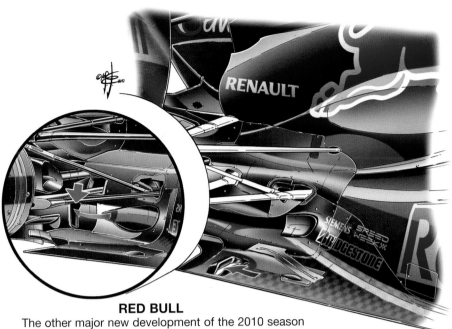

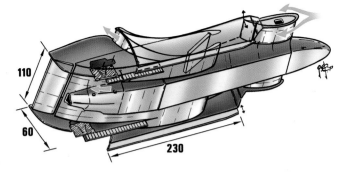

RED BULL

The other major new development of the 2010 season
was the exhaust blow into the lateral channels, created by the ingenious Adrian Newey. He took up once more the concept of blow into the diffusers,
first introduced way back in 1983 by Jean Claude Migeot.
The system is discussed in greater depth in the Engines chapter.

ARROWS A2

The Ferrari F10 also had a secret hidden
away under the skin – the 3.5° inclination of
its engine-gearbox group to augment the volume of the double diffuser area. That was
attempted in 1979 by Tony Southgate on the
futuristic Arrows A2 which, in theory, was to
have raced without wings due to the ground
effect produced by the extremely long mini-
skirts, but it turned out to be a real disaster.

FERRARI RIMS

Ferrari ably circumvented the ban on fairing applied to the
exterior of the rims by integrating the aerodynamic
devices into the design of their wheels while fully respecting the regulations, which required uniformity of material
in the units' production. It was an advantage no other
team was able to copy because, like the chassis, rims are
subjected to homologation and may not be modified during the season.

MERCEDES-BENZ

To increase top speed and reduce the frontal
section, Mercedes-Benz came up with this
knife edge structure as an arc of protection for
its drivers. The hypothetical advantages were
outweighed by the car being unable to adopt
an effective F-duct system without the sail-
type engine cover. Later, in the development
of the diffusers, the structure also became a
functional element of the F-duct system.

Red Bull was the star of the 2010 season, with 15 pole positions and nine victories in 19 races. This after a 2009 in which it produced the most revolutionary car in the recent history of Formula 1. Hurriedly classified at its presentation as a logical evolution of the preceding RB5, the RB6 confirmed itself to be the most avant garde car of them all, even without the F-duct introduced by McLaren.

It did not stray from the shape of the RB5, but under the skin everything was new, with the majority of its latest developments hidden away at the rear end.

Adrian Newey designed the car around the double diffuser concept and the most interesting thing was that it retained the pull rod layout, which in 2009 had created a number of difficulties for the conversion of the RB5 to such a system.

He did it by redesigning a new, longer gearbox to create more volume for the start of the double diffuser, not lower and wider but narrower and raised with a new position for the differential to free space down low.

Right from its presentation, Red Bull began to field a host of new developments at just about every occasion.

Even at the last pre-season test session at Barcelona a version of the car made its appearance with a longer wheelbase distancing the rear axle by a few centimetres. It was an important modification, because it took a great deal of work.

Another ably camouflaged new development was brought in at Spanish pre-testing: an RB6 with divided exhausts, except that the highest one was only a faithful reproduction on a sticker.

The real one was lower and set notably back in a position considered risky, because it was extremely close to the rear tyre. But it was a feature that turned out to be a great advantage for the better exploitation of the rear aerodynamics.

An additional small intake set even further back appeared at the third race in Malaysia to help to blow hot air into the channel that was formed between the tyre and the lateral diffuser. In practice, Newey had brought back exhaust blow into the dif-

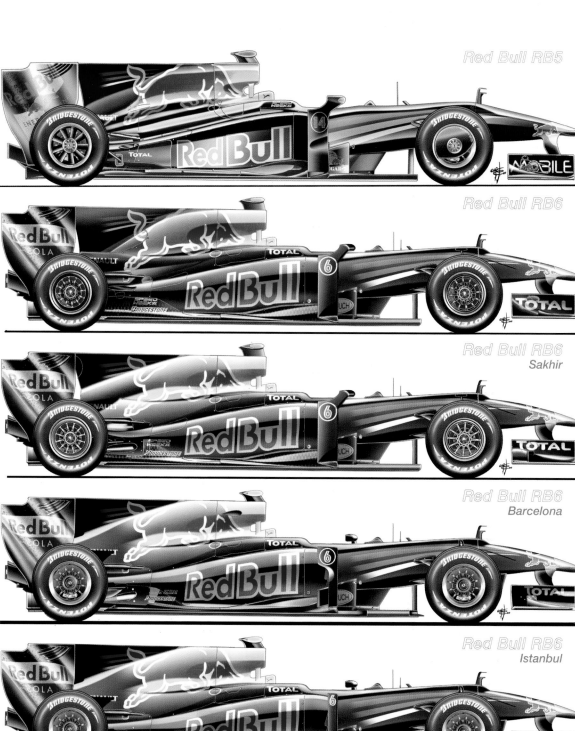

Red Bull RB5

Red Bull RB6

Red Bull RB6
Sakhir

Red Bull RB6
Barcelona

Red Bull RB6
Istanbul

Red Bull RB6
Montreal

CONSTRUCTORS' CLASSIFICATION		
	2009	*2010*
Position	2°	1°

Red Bull RB6
Silverstone

Red Bull RB6
Budapest

Red Bull RB6
Spa

Red Bull RB6
Singapore

Red Bull RB6
Abu Dahbi

to mechanical failures that were completely avoidable, in particular the one that stopped Sebastian Vettel in Australia. He had to retire due to a partially unscrewed right front wheel: during Friday practice in Bahrain there were inklings that the new system for fixing the brake disc hub to the rim was likely to cause problems. It was signalled by brake malfunction on the front left wheel with a damaged disc. The problem repeated itself in Australia, resulting in the right front wheel becoming unlocked. The 2009 system of combining the various elements was changed for 2010 and it was no coincidence that all Friday testing before the GP of Malaysia was spent verifying that the modifications made were the right ones. Development of the car was halted in an effort to recover reliability for the Grand Prix, but the list of new advances introduced at each race was still incredibly long: by way of an example, there were three different front wings in the pits at the first two Grands Prix.

Sometimes, like at the Spanish GP, the mechanics had to assemble more or less a new car on the Thursday evening and night, with double shifts and components that arrived that very day.

As often happens when a car is in a dominant position compared to the opposition, the RB6 was at the centre of controversy due to suspected irregularities.

The first concerned the suspension, which was thought to be using an active solution to ensure the same height from the ground, despite the considerable difference in weight between qualifying and the race.

But the Federation found nothing wrong in the Red Bull layout, although it did come up with a series of clarifications to stop hyper-sophisticated and expensive projects in an effort to get around the regulations.

At the request of the Federation, in Turkey Red Bull had to modify some details that did not respect

fusers' lateral channels, which had not been used for almost 20 years. It was a technique that was continually evolved during the season and copied bit by bit by almost all the other teams. For better or worse, Red Bull was the great protagonist, even with strategic mistakes and some minor problems of unreliability, which helped Ferrari make the comeback that livened up the championship so much.

During the first two races, two victories were thrown away due

the regulations using components that arrived on the Friday night.

There was also controversy over the excessive flexing of the front wing and the bib splitter of the T-tray, brought to light in TV pictures, especially those of the Hungarian GP.

In that case, too, the RB6 passed all the Federation's technical checks, including those at the subsequent Grand Prix of Belgium over the static loads to which these elements were subjected became more severe (see the chapter on 2010 regulations). The fact is that Newey's car was a blend of extreme solutions that were well brought together using methods that required a great deal of research, like the use of the carbon fibre skin that enabled the team to obviate the verification obstacles, the set-up of the car and the co-relation with its aerodynamics.

The RB6's rake, with the front low and the rear decidedly high, raised a few eyebrows, but it was perfectly married to low aerodynamics in which the exhaust blow took on the role of a sort of thermal mini-skirt that made the diffuser efficient again, keeping the car higher off the ground compared to the opposition.

That technology was fully exploited at the Grand Prix of Hungary, where they could take maximum advantage of the hot blow provided by a special mapping of the engine with ignition delay, which allowed the flow of petrol in the exhausts also during the off throttle phase with the successive combustion of the latter. Developed by Renault technicians, the solution was later introduced at Valencia but it needed further development. There was some difficulty in the debut of the F-duct, which also took place in Turkey.

The fact is that with such an extreme car it was exceedingly difficult to find the space for channelling, which had to return to the cockpit to enable the driver to then operate the system with his hand.

The RB6's only defect was its chronically low top speed compared to the other leading cars, which was completely compensated for by the greater speed

through the fast corners.
An astute observer of new developments brought in on his adversaries cars, including those of the second level, Newey adopted the TV camera position down low inside the pillars that supported the front wing at the British GP and then the F-duct blow in the main plane instead of the flap,

which had been used by Force India and Sauber for some time. There were only two examples of the new front wing for Silverstone and they arrived late, which created some controversy: when Vettel damaged his, the team simply took the wing off Mark Webber's car when it was about to take to the track to check its

suitability.
Red Bull tried vertical front brake calipers instead of prone units during the Japanese GP weekend and they were retained for the race. It was an experiment for possible use on the 2011 car, which was then dropped for the subsequent Grands Prix of Korea, Brazil and Abu Dhabi.

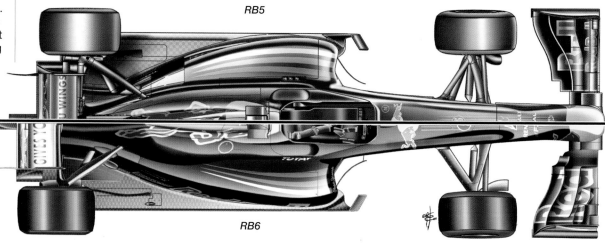

RB5

RB6

TOP VIEW COMPARISON
The Red Bull RB6 was a logical evolution of the RB5 adapted to the different wheelbase dimensions, which were in turn associated with the increased size of the fuel tank. The general shape of the two cars was practically identical, except for the more ample channelling in the front of the chassis and the position of the exhausts, which then underwent a continuous and important evolution during the season.

FRONT VIEW
Note the V-shaped protrusion in the upper part of the chassis, with evident aerodynamic benefits in air flow management in that area. The wide, flat nose shape was unchanged and it retained a main plane combined with a double flap and other upper deck flaps.

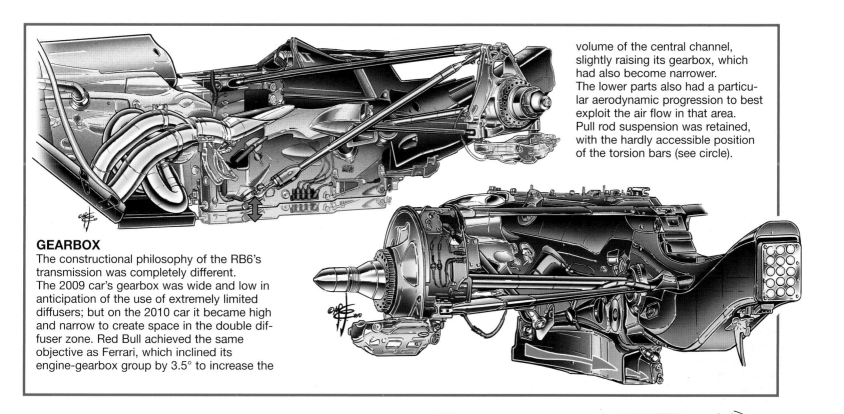

volume of the central channel, slightly raising its gearbox, which had also become narrower.
The lower parts also had a particular aerodynamic progression to best exploit the air flow in that area. Pull rod suspension was retained, with the hardly accessible position of the torsion bars (see circle).

GEARBOX

The constructional philosophy of the RB6's transmission was completely different.
The 2009 car's gearbox was wide and low in anticipation of the use of extremely limited diffusers; but on the 2010 car it became high and narrow to create space in the double diffuser zone. Red Bull achieved the same objective as Ferrari, which inclined its engine-gearbox group by 3.5° to increase the

SAKHIR

For the opening race at Sakhir, the Red Bull exhausts were moved lower to blow into the channel between the tyres and the lateral extractor planes, improving efficiency.
To draw attention away from that move at the last pre-season test session at Barcelona the old position was painted on with an air brush.

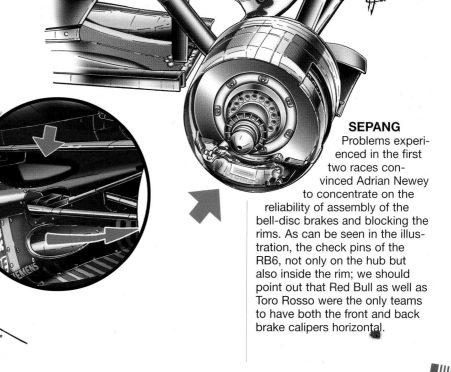

SEPANG

Problems experienced in the first two races convinced Adrian Newey to concentrate on the reliability of assembly of the bell-disc brakes and blocking the rims. As can be seen in the illustration, the check pins of the RB6, not only on the hub but also inside the rim; we should point out that Red Bull as well as Toro Rosso were the only teams to have both the front and back brake calipers horizontal.

FRONT CALIPERS

Red Bull and Toro Rosso were the only two teams that fitted horizontal brake callipers, a technique introduced by Adrian Newey when he was at McLaren, but now dropped by the Woking team.

BLOW: SHANGHAI-BARCELONA

Throughout the season, Red Bull continued to modify the position of its exhausts and their blow into the lateral channels.
This illustration compares the system introduced in China and the one in Spain (see circle). In Shanghai, there was a small vertical window in the central area of the channel, which had two tasks: to suck the flow of hot air away from the rear tyres and, at the same time, to direct it to the inside of the diffuser's lateral channels. But in Barcelona there was a real RB6 revolution: only the front and rear wings were the same as those in China, while all the rest was new.
New sidepods in both their initial and terminal areas, with a much flared and low section (1).
The position of the exhausts (2) was also different and the blow in front of the rear wheels was new and clearly of the McLaren school.

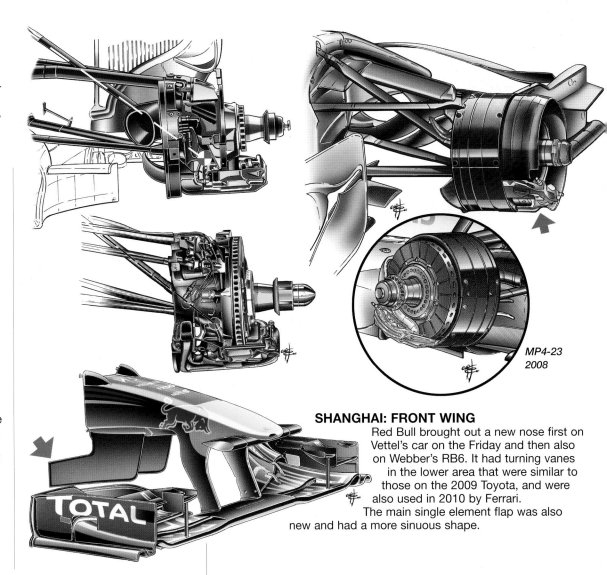

MP4-23 2008

SHANGHAI: FRONT WING

Red Bull brought out a new nose first on Vettel's car on the Friday and then also on Webber's RB6. It had turning vanes in the lower area that were similar to those on the 2009 Toyota, and were also used in 2010 by Ferrari.
The main single element flap was also new and had a more sinuous shape.

MONACO: WING

Red Bull adapted the wing it took to Monaco to the type used by McLaren the previous year, with a considerable blow into the principal plane that ended on the trailing edge as if there were two separate planes, in that way producing more downforce.

1

2

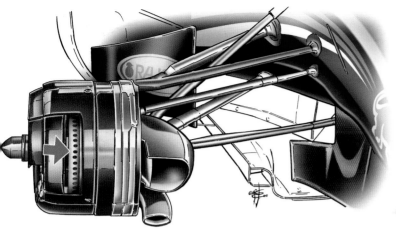

BRAKES

The RB6 admitted a broken brake disc, which had more ample holes at Barcelona. These holes were used during Thursday practice at Monaco, but on the Saturday other discs were fitted that were similar to Ferrari's.

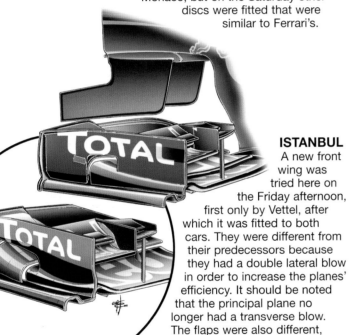

ISTANBUL

A new front wing was tried here on the Friday afternoon, first only by Vettel, after which it was fitted to both cars. They were different from their predecessors because they had a double lateral blow in order to increase the planes' efficiency. It should be noted that the principal plane no longer had a transverse blow. The flaps were also different, because for the first time they could be adjusted by the driver.

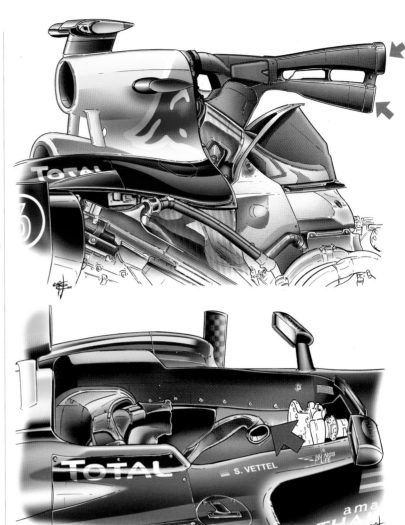

ISTANBUL: F-DUCT

The F-duct made its first appearance on the Red Bull at Istanbul. It was a system similar to McLaren's without the feed intake in the front of the chassis, but made inside a section of the engine air intake. The driver operated it with his left hand. On the Saturday morning all the components of the F-duct system were taken off and the two RB6s were transformed into passive cars, with a new rear wing that had various planes and end plates modified; and it arrived just in time for qualifying. They worked well, although the suspension on Vettel's car did not, because its roll bar broke.

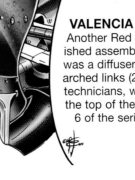

VALENCIA

Another Red Bull revolution happened here, where the mechanics finished assembling the cars at 2am: among the many new developments was a diffuser that was completely different in the upper area, with arched links (2) between the middle plates that, according to the team's technicians, would ensure less pitch sensitivity: the modification (1) to the top of the lateral channels had already appeared in diffuser number 6 of the series taken to Canada.

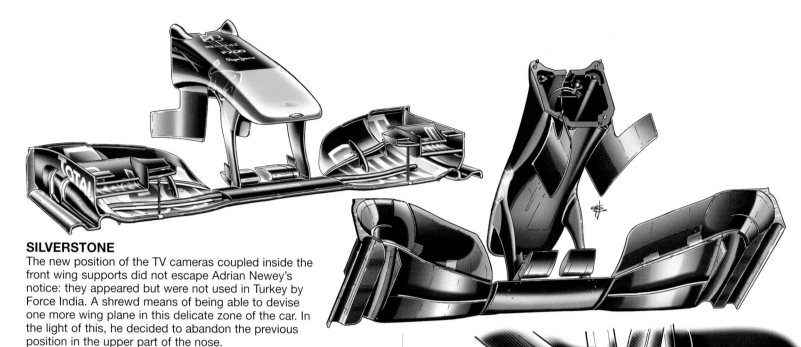

SILVERSTONE

The new position of the TV cameras coupled inside the front wing supports did not escape Adrian Newey's notice: they appeared but were not used in Turkey by Force India. A shrewd means of being able to devise one more wing plane in this delicate zone of the car. In the light of this, he decided to abandon the previous position in the upper part of the nose.

Viewed from down below, it can be clearly seen how the TV cameras functioned as a flap (neutral) in the central section of the main plane. The adjustment of the flap was also new but was not on the other available wing. The end plates had two vertical windows instead of the single unit and the main plane was also different.

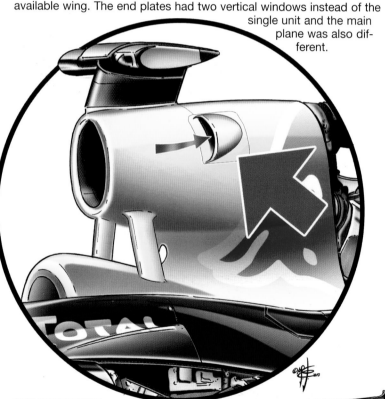

SPA-FRANCORCHAMPS

Fully revealed, the fixing of the Brembo discs, which permit the elimination of the bell with tightening nuts and, therefore, reduce the vortices inside the brake air intake. This was a feature introduced some time earlier by the Italian brake manufacturer, first for Ferrari and then their other client teams.

SILVERSTONE: F-DUCT

There was a brief experiment using Vettel's car on the Friday morning, but it only lasted a few laps. It concerned the F-duct feed from small "ears" positioned at the sides of the air box to try and avoid choking the engine cover air intake.

FRONT WING

Red Bull also took this new wing to Spa, with four stiffeners between the two flaps, but they were not even fitted to the cars except to pass scrutineering on the Thursday.

The centre of the nose was pre-Silverstone, with the TV cameras fixed to the sides of the nose point.

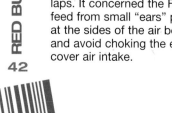

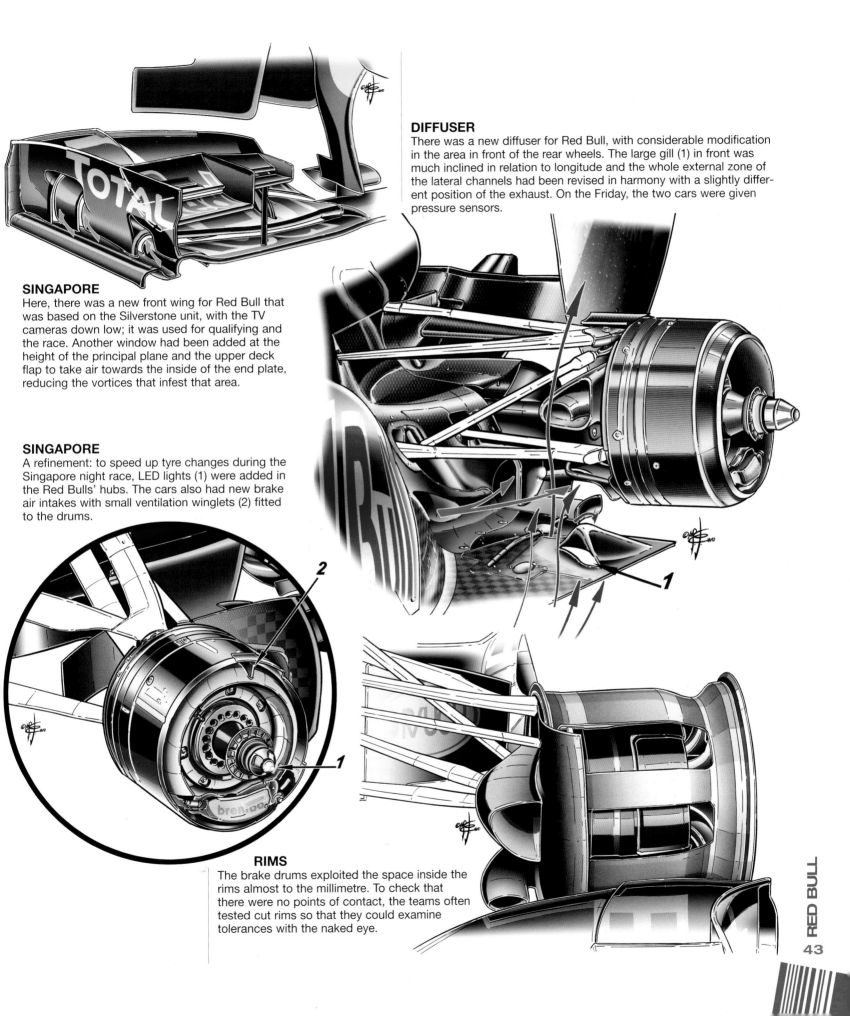

DIFFUSER

There was a new diffuser for Red Bull, with considerable modification in the area in front of the rear wheels. The large gill (1) in front was much inclined in relation to longitude and the whole external zone of the lateral channels had been revised in harmony with a slightly different position of the exhaust. On the Friday, the two cars were given pressure sensors.

SINGAPORE

Here, there was a new front wing for Red Bull that was based on the Silverstone unit, with the TV cameras down low; it was used for qualifying and the race. Another window had been added at the height of the principal plane and the upper deck flap to take air towards the inside of the end plate, reducing the vortices that infest that area.

SINGAPORE

A refinement: to speed up tyre changes during the Singapore night race, LED lights (1) were added in the Red Bulls' hubs. The cars also had new brake air intakes with small ventilation winglets (2) fitted to the drums.

RIMS

The brake drums exploited the space inside the rims almost to the millimetre. To check that there were no points of contact, the teams often tested cut rims so that they could examine tolerances with the naked eye.

SINGAPORE - SUZUKA

Red Bull retained its new rear wing introduced in Singapore and it escaped observation. As with McLaren, Red Bull opted for the more efficient F-duct blow into the main plane instead of into the flap. New also the beam wing, arrow-shaped in the central zone.

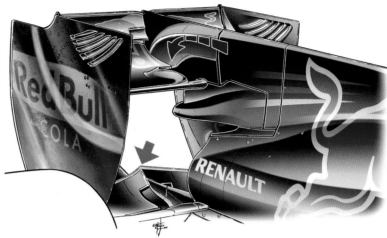

YEONGAM

Red Bull went back to prone brake calipers for the Korean GP, but introduced a new cooling intake that was a mix of several previous units. The new component had one single intake with "ears", which they also used at Suzuka where the calipers were vertical, because the small intake (1) had been eliminated. And the small deflector fin (2) reappeared after its Singapore introduction, while the single intake (4) was different to the Suzuka unit (3). A number of aerodynamic devices (5) of the Renault school were also added.

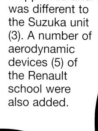

Yeongam

SUZUKA

There was an important RB6 development in Japan.
After many problems had been caused by the prone position of the front brake calipers, which by that time were only being used by Red Bull and Toro Rosso, Adrian Newey allowed himself to be convinced that he should adopt the classic vertical units. These ensured greater reliability and reduced knock-off difficulties. But it was an experiment put to one side for the subsequent Grand Prix of Korea.

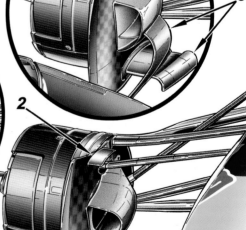

Suzuka

Singapore

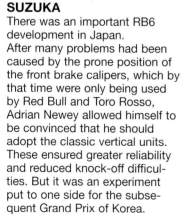

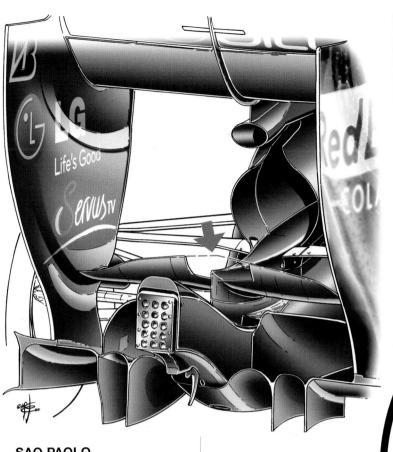

ABU DAHBI

Another feature prohibited for the 2011 season was the double diffuser, but not the low blow of the exhausts. This illustration shows in detail how the Red Bull's blow went under the lateral channels that cross a vertical window in the central channel. It was a method also used on the Ferrari, but with a horizontal opening in the passage between the stepped plane and the central channels.

SAO PAOLO

This is not a new solution, but one carried out on the Friday on Vettel's car. The team had cut the central section of the lower plane to return to the normal version, as on Webber's car.

ALETTONE POSTERIORE

There was a surprise on the Saturday morning when Red Bull fitted a different wing to the one used on the Friday, with greater aerodynamic load and blow directly into the main plane. This time, though, the plane had a central "hole" that turned this single unit into a bi-plane at the trailing edge, a plane that was introduced at Monaco.

Sakhir

SAKHIR - ABU DAHBI

As with Ferrari, the Red Bull cars were subjected
to careful analysis with 3D animation that followed the
development of the car throughout the season.
These two frames synthesise the aerodynamic evolution of the RB6,
from the start of the season to the last race.

Abu Dahbi

For the second consecutive season, McLaren was able to precede Ferrari in the constructors' championship by coming second to Red Bull in 2010 – they came third behind Brawn GP and Red Bull in 2009 – with an MP4-25 that was packed with new content and technical developments, but they still had to kneel before Adrian Newey's Red Bull RB7. The McLaren was a futuristic project by Tim Goss and Paddy Lowe in which the F-duct, called the F-flap at Woking, was the most apparent and copied, but there were many other developments that are more or less easy to identify.

The first, which was macroscopic, was the car's wheelbase dimensions. Even at first glance it immediately appeared the longest of all: well beyond 25 cm more than the Red Bull and about 18 cm more than the Ferrari.

The aerodynamics were carefully fashioned with components like the front wing, the origins of which dated back to developments introduced during the second part of the previous season on the MP4-24.

The choice of a long wheelbase was carefully considered and was not only associated with the unavoidable increase in fuel tank size. A very long gearbox was produced and a suspension layout with the front wishbone arms much inclined forward, to be able to introduce the double diffuser as far ahead as possible after the Federation freed them for the 2010 season.

Nevertheless, this choice was at the basis of the whole project, but it soon turned out to be a real boomerang at its first track test. The enormous volume of the double diffuser created a substantial amount of downforce, but also extremely critical handling in relation to its height from the ground.

To avoid this problem, they had to try to keep the car's distance from the ground as constant as possible with a very rigid suspension set-up, and that made the car's handling extremely nervous on bumps and kerbs.

The McLaren lost one of its positive points, which was the car's ability to hit the kerbs without losing its equilibrium.

CONSTRUCTORS' CLASSIFICATION		
	2009	2010
Position	3°	2°

McLAREN

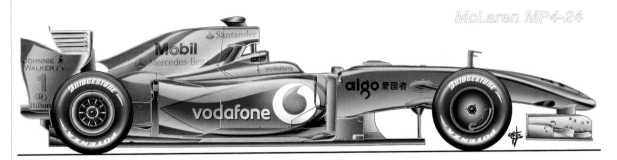

McLaren MP4-24

McLaren MP4-25

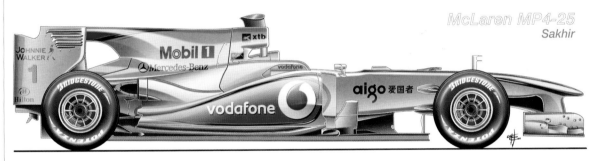

McLaren MP4-25
Sakhir

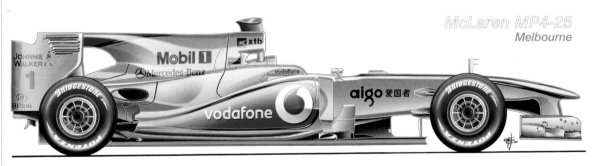

McLaren MP4-25
Melbourne

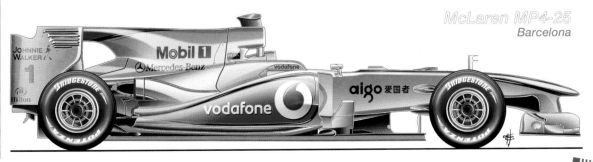

McLaren MP4-25
Barcelona

It took almost half the season to resolve the problem and make the MP4-25 less twitchy.

But let's get back to the F-flap, which set a trend in 2010, and was a project the team began to study in 2008. In 2009, the blown main plane made its debut at Monaco with a divided trailing edge, which virtually transformed the single element into a double, working its way around the regulation limitation.

At that time, the purpose was to increase in downforce, while that of the F-flap was precisely the opposite – to reduce resistance at full speed.

There was always blow in both the plane – in this case the flap – and the rear, the flow of which was regulated by an air valve dating to the cold war aeronautical patent.

McLaren was the only team to use the F-flap at Monaco, combined with a high downforce wing with a main plane that was split at the exit. Strangely, though, it was not used on - Lewis Hamilton's car at Monza. We have devoted more space to this ingenious advance – even if it was based on a borderline interpretation of the regulations – in the New Developments chapter.

The development of the MP4-25 was incredible, second only to that of the Red Bull.

There were new features at just about every Grand Prix and they are given here in a list provided by McLaren.

They were tested on the Friday to be approved by the drivers. Paint was often used to verify the usefulness of the new elements evidencing on the track the progression of the air flow.

A new diffuser with longitudinal end plates to increase the volume of the hole was tried out in the last pre-season test which, curiously, was then first used during a GP by Renault and not McLaren.

And at almost every Grand Prix McLaren had a new ad hoc front wing that was different from its predecessor.

The team often used the terminal parts of the asymmetric sidepods, adopting bigger opening on the left 'pod for the dissipation of hot air.

The MP4-25 was really fast in racing order with a full fuel tank, but due to the outstanding

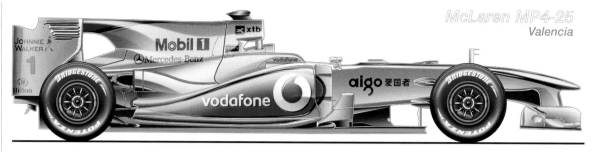

McLaren MP4-25
Valencia

McLaren MP4-25
Silverstone

McLaren MP4-25
Hockenheim

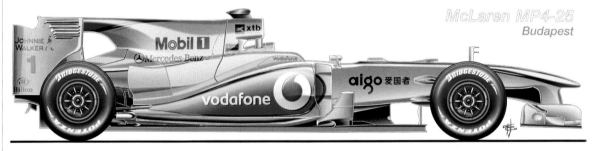

McLaren MP4-25
Budapest

McLaren MP4-25
Monza Button

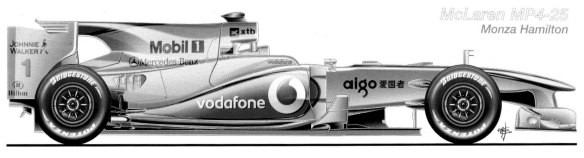

McLaren MP4-25
Monza Hamilton

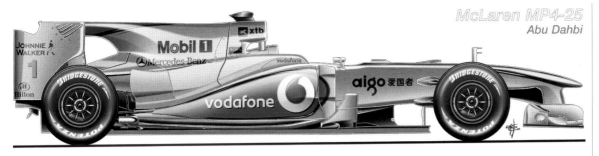

exploitation of the F-flap the car yielded less in qualifying set-up, where Red Bull dominated the season by taking 15 pole positions in 19 races.

Confirmation of that situation comes from the team's five victories and just one pole position. Another difficulty for McLaren was its slight delay, compared to the opposition, in introducing blown diffusers, which took place in two stages.

They were the debut in practice at Silverstone and at Hockenheim for the German race. Meanwhile, Ferrari and Renault adopted theirs from the GP of Valencia.

Hamilton and Jenson Button integrated themselves well into the style of driving, with the latter extremely successful in preserving his tyres during the races.

From the technical point of view, the biggest difference was in the use of various materials for the cars' brake discs, with Hamilton the more aggressive and loyal to those of Carbon Industrie and Button Brembo.

The 2009 world champion was also ill at ease during the full exploitation of the hot blow under deceleration, introduced at the Grand Prix of Germany.

A SEASON OF DEVELOPMENTS, RACE-BY-RACE:

Sakhir (final pre-season tests)
Aero: 17
Vehicle: 19
Engine: 4
Front wing elements and mechanism. Improvements to front and rear floor, attendant bodywork, sidepod wing and turning vanes.

Melbourne
Aero: 2
Improvements derived from re-sited mirrors on sidepod wings (shortlived due to imminent regulation changes).

Sepang
Aero: 7

Updated floor – including revisions to the bib. Nosebox improvements.

Shanghai
Aero: 3
Vehicle: 1
Small aerodynamic modifications to the floor.

Barcellona
Aero: 9
Vehicle: 1
Major upgrade to rear wing – and attendant modifications to affected ancillaries. Modifications to floor. Weight reduction programme implemented.

Monaco
Aero: 2
Vehicle: 2

Engine: 1
Circuit-specific braking mods. Steering rack changes – to accommodate Monaco hairpin etc.

Istanbul
Aero: 5
Changes to the rear brake ducts. Medium-downforce F-duct rear wing.

Montreal
Aero: 3
Vehicle: 1
Revised front-wing elements. Minor improvements to floor. Further weight reduction improvements implemented.

Valencia
Aero: 2
Vehicle: 2
Increased cooling capacity for this particular race. More weight saving. New steering rack.

Silverstone
Aero: 7
Vehicle: 3
Engine: 4
Introduced revised floor concept based around the blown diffuser (not raced until Hockenheim). Tested different iterations of front wings and endplates. Improved Mobil 1 fuel. Engine mapping

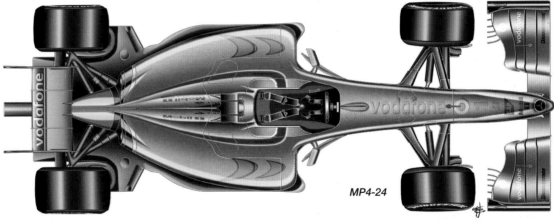

MP4-24

TOP VIEW

In this top view comparison, the design similarities between the MP4-24 and the MP4-25 can be easily seen. The 25 retains its predecessor's nose shape and the initial part of the sidepods. The difference in wheelbase is obvious: 3,480 mm against the 2009 car's 3,228 mm. Note the absence of the cut underbody in front of the rear wheels, which was eliminated already during the 2009 season.

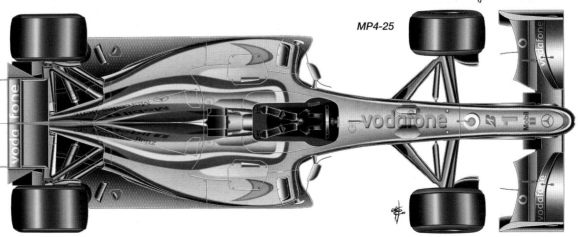

MP4-25

updates. Weight reduction. Brake mods.

Hockenheim
Aero: 5
Engine: 1
Additional mods for introduction of blown diffuser. Engine mapping updates.

Budapest
Aero: 2
Vehicle: 1
Circuit-specific cooling.

Spa
Aero: 8
Vehicle: 2
Engine: 1
New rear wing. Further-modified front wing. Improvements to diffuser. Further engine mapping mods. Suspension modifications.

Monza
Aero: 11
Vehicle: 1
Large circuit-specific upgrade, including Monza-spec rear wing and top-body without F-duct (raced by Lewis – albeit briefly). More floor mods.

Singapore
Aero: 4
New front wing, with revised mainplane, and double-deck nose-splitter.

Suzuka
Aero: 4
Vehicle: 3
Engine: 3
New rear wing introduced but not raced – the F-duct now blows onto the mainplane. More engine mapping improvements introduced. Large-scale weight reduction programme.

Yeongam
Aero: 2
Vehicle: 2
Engine: 2
Mods for Suzuka wing. Further changes to latest iteration of front wing. Engine mapping upgrades. Weight saving.

San Paolo
Aero: 7
Vehicle: 3
Engine: 1
Front-wing and floor upgrade.

Abu Dahbi
Aero: 1
Rear wing upgrade.

According to our reconstruction, the team used a total of seven different front wings, eight rears, nine diffusers, six bodies (often asymmetric in the terminal area of the sidepods), five different exhausts and seven modifications of the F-flap system.

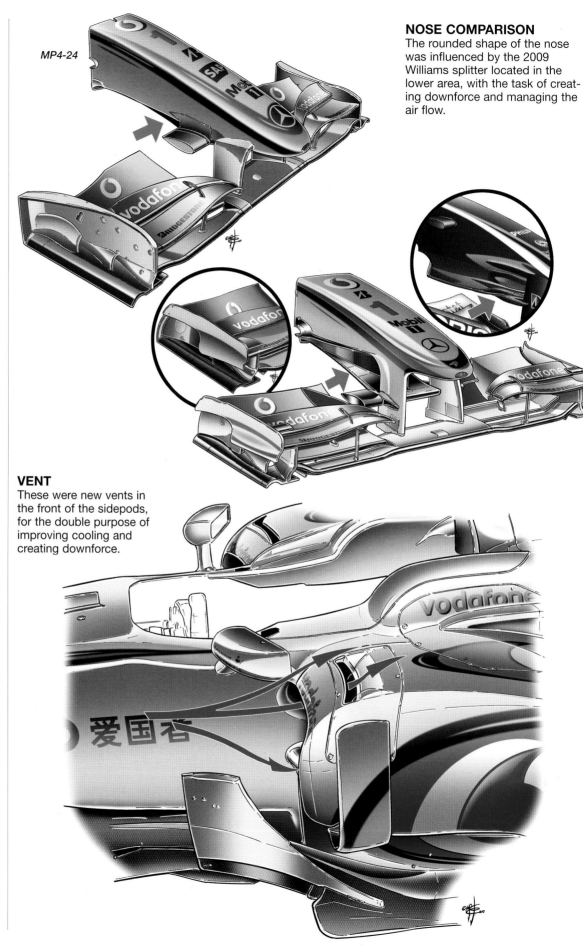

MP4-24

NOSE COMPARISON
The rounded shape of the nose was influenced by the 2009 Williams splitter located in the lower area, with the task of creating downforce and managing the air flow.

VENT
These were new vents in the front of the sidepods, for the double purpose of improving cooling and creating downforce.

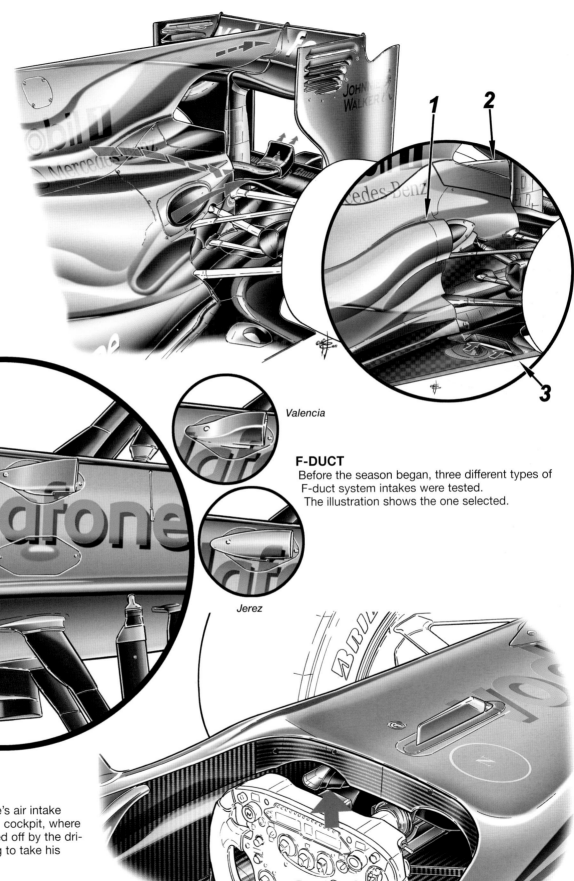

SAKHIR

Here, the McLaren had new side-pods to further improve cooling, incorporating a feature that dates back to the second half of 2009 (1). The lower part of the fin (2) was also modified.

The blow in the zone ahead of the rear wheels (3) was also new, even if it is a copy of a solution introduced by Red Bull the previous year.

Barcelona

Valencia

F-DUCT

Before the season began, three different types of F-duct system intakes were tested.
The illustration shows the one selected.

Jerez

CHANNELLING

The channelling started at the nose's air intake and crossed the entire chassis and cockpit, where a hole was positioned to be blocked off by the driver's left elbow to avoid him having to take his hands off the steering wheel.

ENGINE AIR INTAKE

In this detail, which is normally not easy to see, one can understand how difficult it was for the other teams to copy McLaren's F-duct. In fact, this feature was integrated into the MP4-25'basic project: note how the engine cover area perfectly holds all the channelling. The one down low on the right comes from the intake in the front area of the chassis, goes through the whole monocoque with a substantial section. The two that have been paired cool the hydraulic equipment, while the engine air intake was divided in two so that the lower section fed the engine and the upper blew into the wing flap.

F-DUCT LAYOUT

This table groups together all the ingredients invented by McLaren to reduce downforce in a straight. It was thought this variation was operated by the driver's left knee (see layout), but Paddy Lowe pointed out that control was by the left elbow so that the driver did not have to take his hands off the steering wheel. When the hole was closed (1) in the channelling that began at the intake at the front of the chassis (indicated with an arrow), the air was forced inside the large fin deviating the flow (2) to its inside towards the upper area of the wing. That made the flap stall as it has a slotted vent visible in the illustration below. The driver does not close the hole in a corner, so that the air enters the cockpit but does not influence the flow that normally goes to the lower part of the wing, increasing the diffuser's efficiency.

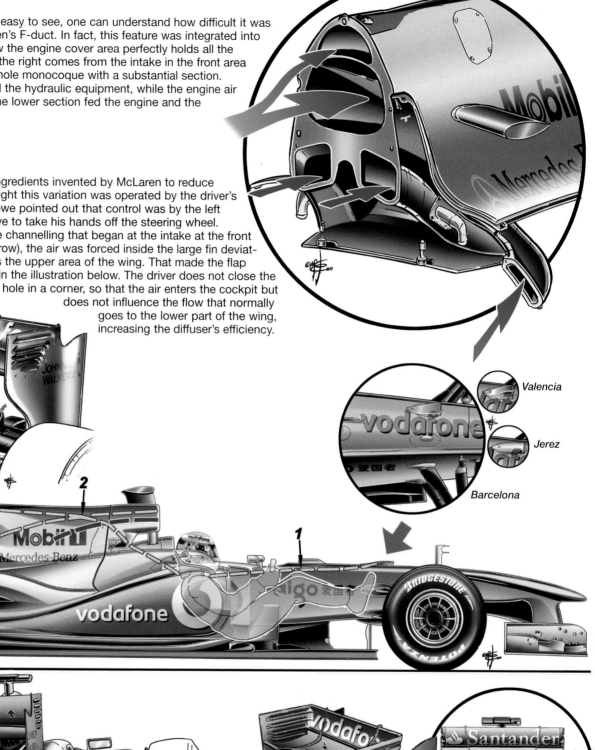

Valencia

Jerez

Barcelona

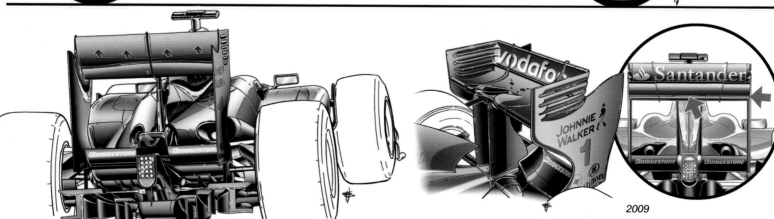

2009

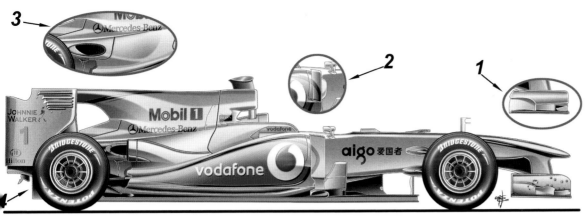

There was a new aerodynamic package for the first race of the season, which had:
1) new front wing end plates;
2) "boomerangs" in front of the sidepods;
3) a vent in the exhausts area to improve cooling;
4) a new diffuser.

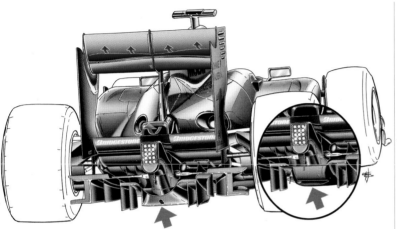

DIFFUSORE

There was criticism of the new McLaren diffuser (see circle) because the window through which to access the starter had become a blow, like a further diffuser. The development had been adopted by Brawn GP in 2009, but the FIA judged it irregular and asked for a modification for Melbourne.

DIFFUSER

As forecast, McLaren had to modify the central area of its diffuser planes, notably reducing the horizontal opening, which was not justified to act as an access to the engine starting system.

SEPANG

This was the third new diffuser in three races for McLaren. It had an upwards curved area at its periphery (1), a wider channel in the areas at the sides of the wheels (2) and a horizontal Gurney flap lower down. The central zone (4) was unchanged, except that it was modified as early as Melbourne to respect the regulations. In the circle is the comparison with the diffuser used in Australia.

FRONT END PLATES

FIA asked McLaren to eliminate the bib splitter of the end plates, in practice adding in the rounded fillets (shown in yellow) to respect the regulations of a 5mm radius in all the peripheral areas of the end plates.

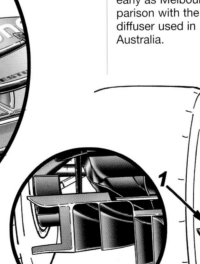

BARCELONA

Another substantial wing development was introduced by McLaren the previous year at Monaco, with an enormous hole in the central area of the principal plane. It continued to the interior of the plane until it ended having been divided at the trailing edge to create, in the view from the rear, the effect of two separate planes in addition to the traditional flap, which continued to have a cut to permit the use of the F-duct.

FRONT WING

Another version of the front wing, still based on four planes: the new element concerned the split end plates in two pieces to improve air flow in this delicate area of the car.

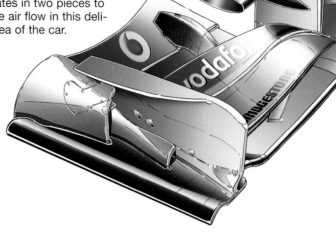

MONACO

McLaren retained the new diffuser introduced in Barcelona and inspired by that of Renault, with two longitudinal planes to further widen the gap in the central area and improve air extraction in that zone. The lateral channel (1) started much further ahead and almost formed a single plane with the end, which was slightly more arched.
There was a new flap in the central zone (2), which also had another blow (3) in the area under the deformable structure.

REAR WING

There was a deep evolution of the McLaren's rear wing, with its main plane divided at the trailing edge, first brought in during the previous season at Monaco. The MP4-25's blow had been doubled making another two holes at the sides of the large central intake to increase air flow directed to the main plane's interior and then exiting with two distinct apertures in the rear.

ISTANBUL

Here, McLaren had two new front wings that were different from each other, particularly in the terminal area of the lateral end plates, based on those introduced in Spain.
The illustration shows the one used in the race, while in the circle is the wing tested on the Friday with the help of paints to highlight the flow on the track.

SILVERSTONE

McLaren's wing at the British circuit was really innovative and was also retained for the race. The division of the end plates was even more evident than in previous versions, of which it only kept the modified external end plate: another was added, but was moved about 25 cm inwards. But the most interesting aspect was that the main plane was divided into two sections to create an intermediate seal.
To decisively separate the air flow between the internal and external parts of the front wheels.

LOW EXHAUSTS

There was a rather unhappy debut for McLaren's low exhausts on the Friday at Silverstone: they did not pass the track test, at least not at first. Note the cooling openings that took the place of the high exhausts' vents. The low blow was slightly directed towards the outside of the lateral channels.

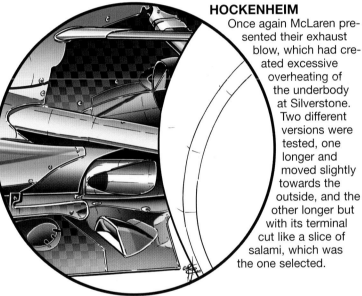

HOCKENHEIM

Once again McLaren presented their exhaust blow, which had created excessive overheating of the underbody at Silverstone. Two different versions were tested, one longer and moved slightly towards the outside, and the other longer but with its terminal cut like a slice of salami, which was the one selected.

BUDAPEST

McLaren continued with its lengthened exhausts and the internal section of the wheel modified and covered with French company Pyrossic's anti-heat material, a mix of ceramics, glass and resin.

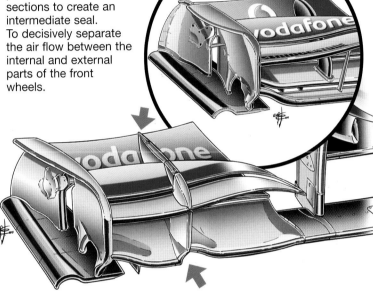

BRAKE AIR INTAKES

New aerodynamic devices were placed in the lower area of the brake air intakes to separate the turbulence generated by the wheels from the flow directed towards the sidepods.

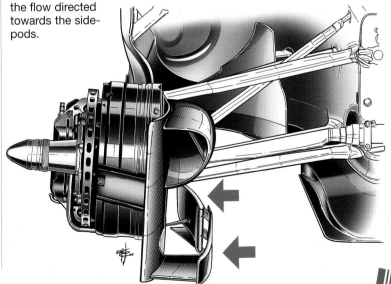

SPA-FRANCORCHAMPS

Another new McLaren front wing appeared in Belgium. It was based on the Silverstone unit but was further modified in the lateral end plates area, which had a wider external section and a different vertical blow of the kind to make the rounded link with the flap intervene. The turning vanes as did the teeth in the lower part of the plane. The wing was used by Jenson Button, while Lewis Hamilton opted for the wing brought in at Valencia, which ensured greater load.

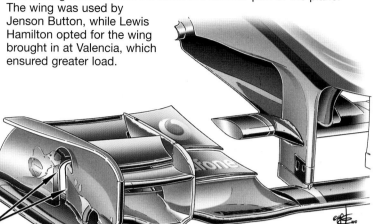

SINGAPORE

McLaren's new front wing for Singapore was extremely sophisticated. It was created on the basics of the main plane introduced at Silverstone, which already had the lower step to more decisively separate the three sections: they were the central unit with the neutral part imposed by the regulations; the middle vane to direct air flow towards the rear of the car; and the external, that expelled air towards the outside of the wheel. An additional middle vane was introduced in Singapore, integrated with the upper deck flap and aligned within the interior of the wheel to better direct the air towards the external part of the tyre and improve the air extraction from the front wing, making it more efficient. The red arrow indicates the doubling of the plane in the zone under the nose to improve the downforce effect in that area, which is otherwise neutral due to the presence of the section of zero incidence required by the Federation.

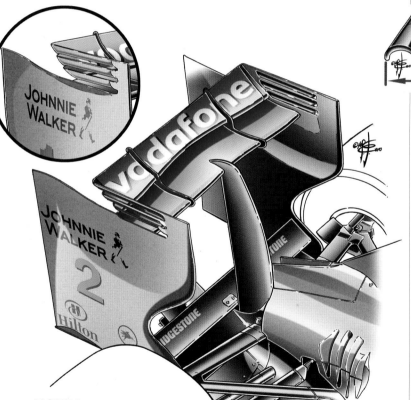

MONZA

Hamilton chose an extreme wing for Monza without an F-duct but with reduced chord planes. And the support was only made of a single element. Note that the lateral end plates were those of the wing used the previous year, but with different planes. The terminal area of the engine cover was also new and without a dorsal fin.

SUZUKA

The new rear wing that was part of the McLaren MP4-25's new developments but was not used in either qualifying or the race due to a lack of data following Hamilton's accident, and the suppression of Friday practice. The F-duct blow was moved from the flap to the main plane – as on the Renault – not to improve the efficiency of the system but due to the impossibility of making it work suitably together with the flap that came in on the new wing. Also note the new end plates with oblique, Red Bull-type gills in place of horizontals (see old shape in the circle).

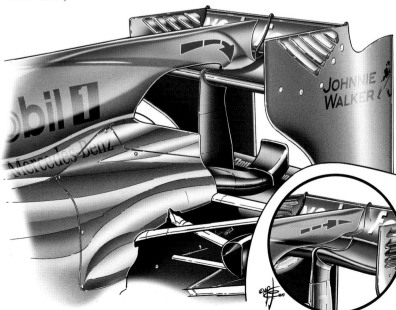

REAR SUSPENSION

This illustration clearly shows how the front wishbone arms of the rear suspension were much inclined forward, so that the hole for the double diffuser could start as far ahead as possible.

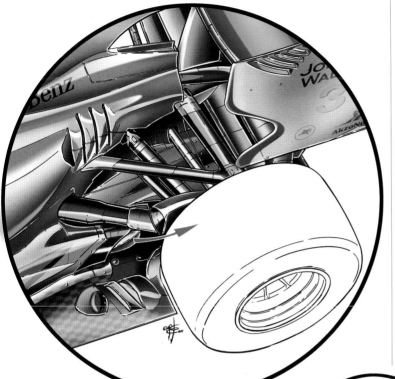

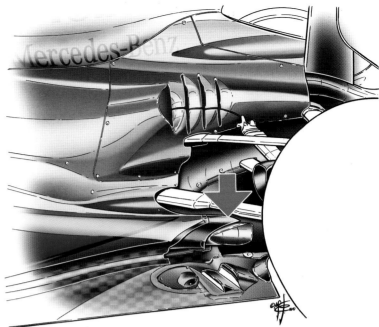

KOREA

The aerodynamic package for Korea included the retention of the lengthened exhaust terminal, which first appeared at Suzuka and also needed a slight lengthening of the body (in carbon fibre) as shown by the arrow. The engine cover was asymmetric and the gills were only on the left side of the car.

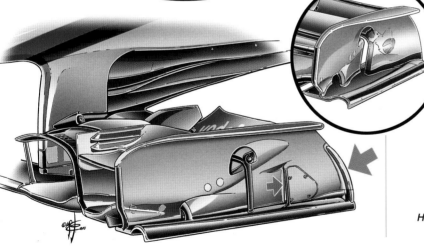

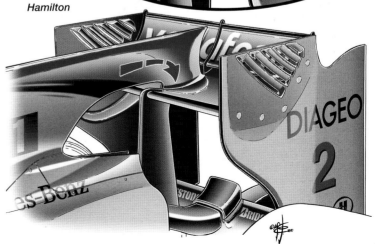

Button

Hamilton

NEW FRONT WING

Another new front wing for McLaren. An additional vertical gill appeared in the end plates, while in their trailing edge a vertical Gurney flap was added to recoup a little downforce.

ABU DAHBI

On the Friday, the two McLaren drivers conducted comparative tests with two different rear wings.
Hamilton used the revised and corrected version of the Suzuka unit with oblique gills in the lateral end plates à la Red Bull and the blow in the main plane.
Button tested the high downforce unit with blow into the flap.
The Hamilton wing was the one used for qualifying and the race.

The Ferrari F10 season was a cliff hanger on the technical front that featured an incredible comeback – partly aided by Red Bull's mistakes – in which the whole team was involved, swept along by the will and stubbornness of Fernando Alonso, who had always believed in the redemption of the Rosse.

During winter testing, the F10 was at the centre of attention for two key reasons: one was its engine, which was inclined 3.5°, and the other its rims with aerodynamic faring that had sidestepped the limitations imposed by the Federation in that area. The victory of the F10 at the world championship's opening race made people think that perhaps 2010 was going to be the year for the Alonso-Ferrari duo. But, unfortunately, it was soon clear that Ferrari had become the third force in F1 on a purely technical level, behind Red Bull and McLaren. The former because it had fielded the most innovative and, on paper, competitive car, and the latter for having introduced a technical feature that characterised the entire season – the F-duct, which became the way to go for all the leading cars. So began a technical catch-up plan, which was perhaps a little too conservative, and that transformed the F10 project, despite the unique 3.5° engine inclination, to create more precise rear aerodynamics and turn it into the most versatile and effective car of the season; in fact it became the only one able to stand up to the Red Bull Vettel-Webber duo. The technical group directed by Aldo Costa decided that, of the F-duct and the blown exhausts, it would give precedence to the former (GPs of Spain and Turkey) for reasons of simplicity of realisation, postponing to Valencia the debut of the blown exhausts. They needed some intense research work to also achieve the correct thermal insulation of all the components involved – body, underbody and suspension.

The Ferrari comeback culminated in Alonso overtaking Webber in the drivers' championship table after the GP of Korea in what was a disastrous race for Red Bull. To analyse Ferrari's revival, it is necessary to identify its fundamental stages, the first of

Ferrari F60

Ferrari F10

Ferrari F10
Test

Ferrari F10
Sakhir

Ferrari F10
Shanghai

Ferrari F10
Barcelona

CONSTRUCTORS' CLASSIFICATION		
	2009	*2010*
Position	4°	3°

Ferrari F10
Monaco

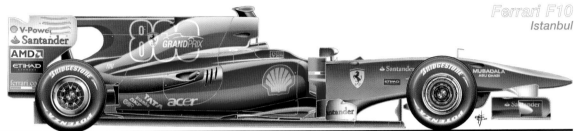

Ferrari F10
Istanbul

Ferrari F10
Valencia

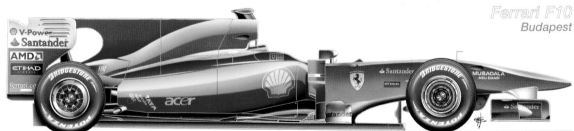

Ferrari F10
Hockenheim

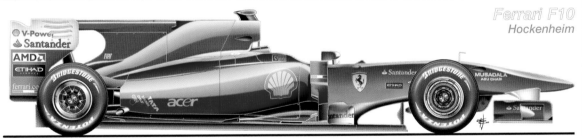

Ferrari F10
Budapest

Ferrari F10
Spa

which took place in Valencia with the introduction of low exhausts; the second happened at Spa with the new rear end that was centred on a diffuser that became a real ground shaker, in part due to a new gearbox casting, although its internal components were unchanged.

This 'box passed its crash test in early July and then made its debut on both cars at Spa, together with the new diffuser. The first appearance of the F-ducts was decisive but not determinate. An experimental version showed up in China and then in the Spanish race, but the advantages of its adoption were not so incisive as that of the other two features.

And perhaps the completion of this project slowed the development of the rest of the F10, which lost ground in relation to the opposition.

If on the one hand Red Bull respected the script that projected it as the absolute protagonist – in both good and bad, throwing precious points to the wind due to mistakes for sporting and technical reasons – on the other hand Ferrari replied with a calmness and confidence that was rather surprising.

The most interesting thing is that the Rosse were able to beat both Red Bull and McLaren over the same terrain, where the two teams had devised new solutions. The Monza victory was due to the supremacy of their F-duct, which was modified ad hoc to adapt it to the rear wing of reduced chord used at the Italian circuit. It turned out that McLaren was beaten with a weapon it had conceived itself, fielding two totally different cars that were a long way from being the best compromise for that track. Hamilton's car had no F-duct at all. The same went for the low exhausts that blew in the area of the diffuser's lateral channels. They were introduced by Red Bull; Ferrari copied them but then took them further, devising a system that was, perhaps, less affected by height variations from the ground, avoiding the partial blow inside those lateral channels.

The F10's aerodynamics seemed highly efficient, but with less downforce compared to that of Red Bull.

Yet you just had to look at the front wings of the season's three leading cars to see that Maranello had selected a different path, aiming very much for efficiency.

The result? Well, perhaps the F10 was less competitive in qualifying, but it showed it was easier and more equilibrated to set up for the various characteristics of the different circuits.

Wearing the tyres less was often a limit at a purely performance level per single lap, but is showed it was a strong point in racing, enabling Alonso to preserve his tyres and deliver a more constant rhythm, also in the final phases of races.

The modifications made during the second half of the season were measured out to avoid creating complications in the little time available during the Friday stints, where the two adversaries Red Bull and McLaren sometimes created 'indigestion' by bringing in a host of new developments but, in the end, benefitting less than expected.

And lastly, while still analysing Ferrari's season, the supremacy of the Brembo braking system must be lauded, with its elements designed ad hoc for the features of the various circuits, which enabled Alonso to be extremely effective and aggressive.

The 8-cylinder Ferrari caused too many worries in the first part of the season, one of the reasons being its slightly higher fuel consumption, but the men from Maranello were even able to recover form this, despite the limitations on engine development imposed by the regulations. The bitter disappointment of Abu Dhabi must not allow anyone to forget that in the end the title went to the best duo: the Red Bull RB6, which was without doubt the most competitive car of recent F1 history, and Sebastian Vettel. However, as a result of Alonso's contribution, the Ferrari F10 pulled off some real miracles.

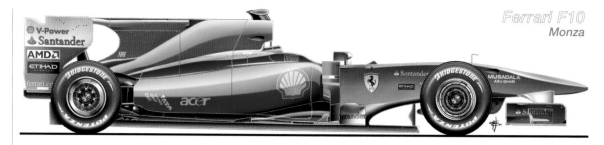

Ferrari F10
Monza

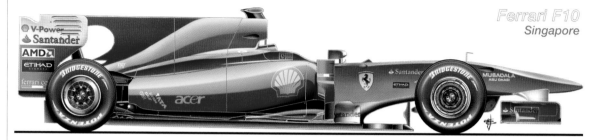

Ferrari F10
Singapore

Ferrari F10
Abu Dahbi

TOP VIEW

At its presentation, the F 10 was clearly "camouflaged", but despite that the differences between it and the end-of-season version of the old F60 were:
1) The nose was higher off the ground and longer.
2) The chassis and, therefore, also the nose adopted the horns in its upper area, originally introduced by Red Bull.

3) As required by the regulations, the front tyres were 20 mm narrower.
4) Horizontal arrow shaped small fins had been placed to the front of the sidepods.
5) The fuel tank was not only longer but exploited the whole 80 cm conceded for its width, as can be construed from the shape of the body.

6) The exhaust exit revealed one of the new features of the F 10, with their collectors upside down to distance the exit from the rear wing area.
7) The F 10 was almost 20 cm longer than the F60 and was mid-way between the Mercedes-Benz, which was the shortest of the top teams' cars, and the longest, the McLaren.

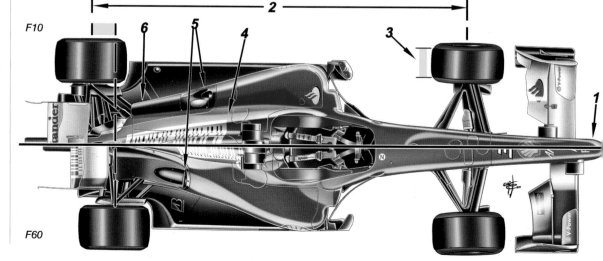

INCLINED ENGINE

The Ferrari F 10 also hid a new feature under its bodywork: its engine had been installed at a 3.5° inclination (2) in order to be able to increase the volume of the double diffusers. The exhausts fitted backwards (1) were renewed so that they could exit before the rear wing.

Note that the dimensions of the fuel tank had increased following the abolition of refuelling, as dictated by the Federation for the 2010 season.

WHEEL NUT

The regulations required that the 2010 cars had to have an automatic but mechanical system to lock the wheel nut: this is how Ferrari did it, with two small levers that emerged the moment the gun stopped tightening of the nut.

3,5°

RIMS

The Ferrari rims were of new concept and did not make their debut until the last pre-season test sessions. They had double rings that were an integral part of the rim design and had been homologated and approved by the Federation, made of a single material as required by the regulations.
On the other hand, the lenticular rim covers of previous seasons were made of carbon fibre. The two rings, which improved the extraction of air, were made of cast magnesium, as were the rest of the rims.
The aerodynamic advantages were such as to justify the more than slight increase in weight.

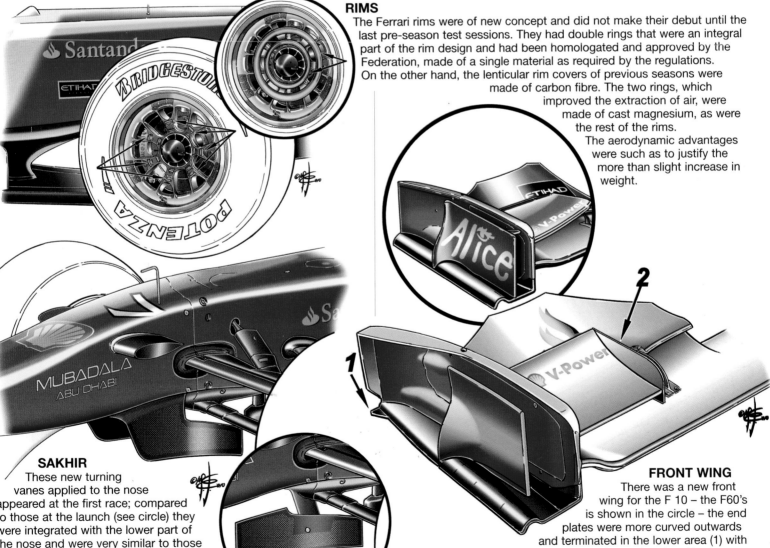

SAKHIR

These new turning vanes applied to the nose appeared at the first race; compared to those at the launch (see circle) they were integrated with the lower part of the nose and were very similar to those used by Toyota in 2009.

FRONT WING

There was a new front wing for the F 10 – the F60's is shown in the circle – the end plates were more curved outwards and terminated in the lower area (1) with a rounded edge. The cascade wing was less twisted and had an interior mini-end plate (2).

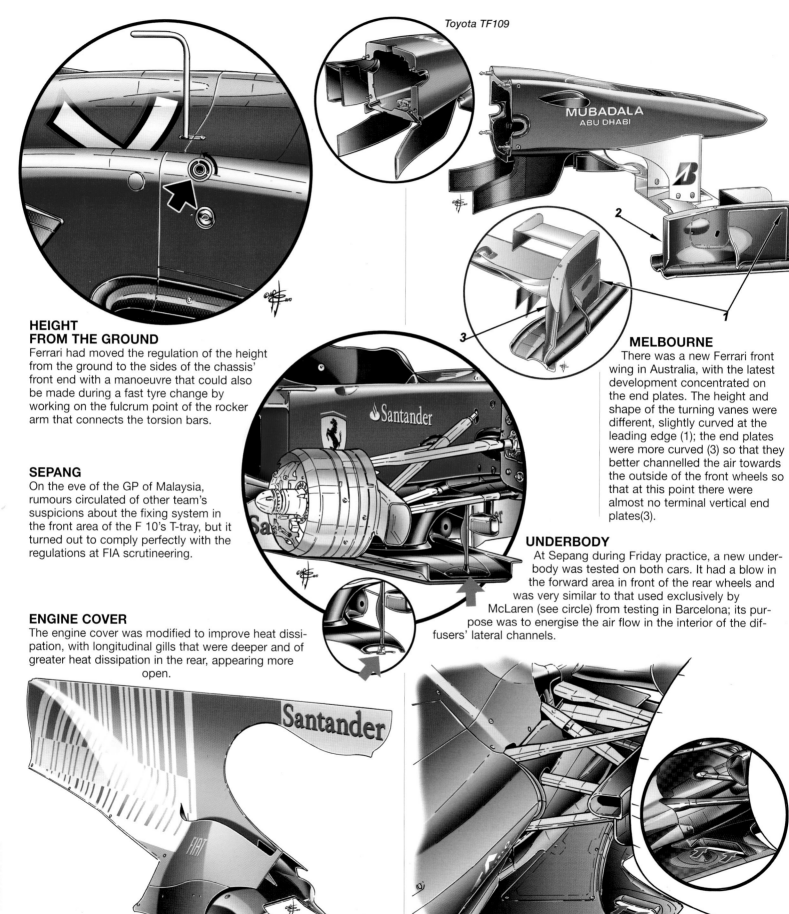

Toyota TF109

HEIGHT FROM THE GROUND

Ferrari had moved the regulation of the height from the ground to the sides of the chassis' front end with a manoeuvre that could also be made during a fast tyre change by working on the fulcrum point of the rocker arm that connects the torsion bars.

SEPANG

On the eve of the GP of Malaysia, rumours circulated of other team's suspicions about the fixing system in the front area of the F 10's T-tray, but it turned out to comply perfectly with the regulations at FIA scrutineering.

ENGINE COVER

The engine cover was modified to improve heat dissipation, with longitudinal gills that were deeper and of greater heat dissipation in the rear, appearing more open.

MELBOURNE

There was a new Ferrari front wing in Australia, with the latest development concentrated on the end plates. The height and shape of the turning vanes were different, slightly curved at the leading edge (1); the end plates were more curved (3) so that they better channelled the air towards the outside of the front wheels so that at this point there were almost no terminal vertical end plates(3).

UNDERBODY

At Sepang during Friday practice, a new under-body was tested on both cars. It had a blow in the forward area in front of the rear wheels and was very similar to that used exclusively by McLaren (see circle) from testing in Barcelona; its purpose was to energise the air flow in the interior of the diffusers' lateral channels.

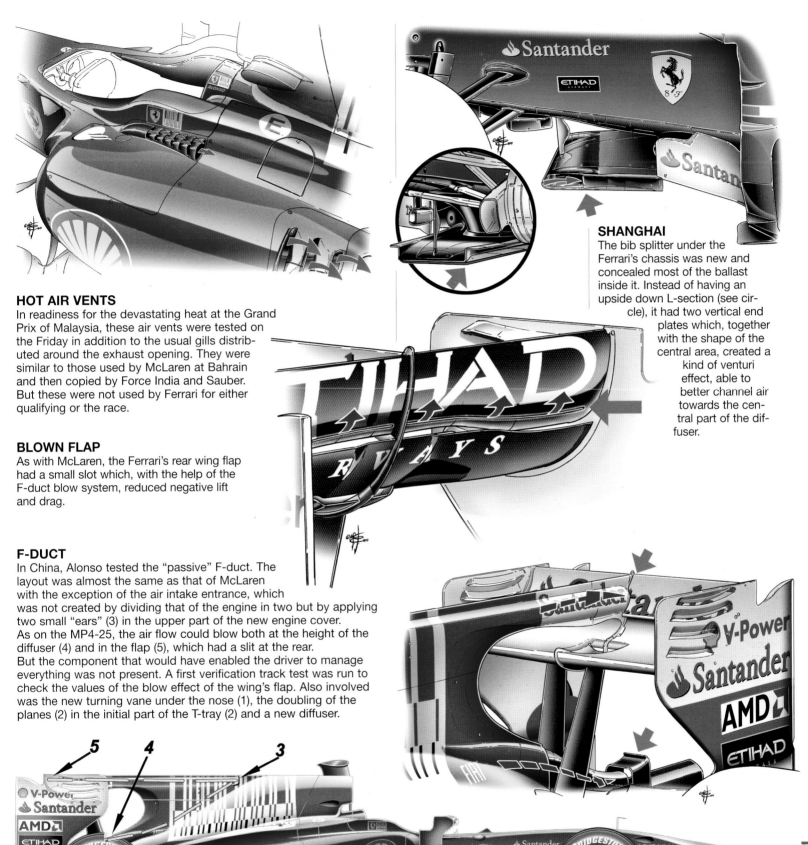

HOT AIR VENTS
In readiness for the devastating heat at the Grand Prix of Malaysia, these air vents were tested on the Friday in addition to the usual gills distributed around the exhaust opening. They were similar to those used by McLaren at Bahrain and then copied by Force India and Sauber. But these were not used by Ferrari for either qualifying or the race.

BLOWN FLAP
As with McLaren, the Ferrari's rear wing flap had a small slot which, with the help of the F-duct blow system, reduced negative lift and drag.

F-DUCT
In China, Alonso tested the "passive" F-duct. The layout was almost the same as that of McLaren with the exception of the air intake entrance, which was not created by dividing that of the engine in two but by applying two small "ears" (3) in the upper part of the new engine cover.
As on the MP4-25, the air flow could blow both at the height of the diffuser (4) and in the flap (5), which had a slit at the rear.
But the component that would have enabled the driver to manage everything was not present. A first verification track test was run to check the values of the blow effect of the wing's flap. Also involved was the new turning vane under the nose (1), the doubling of the planes (2) in the initial part of the T-tray (2) and a new diffuser.

SHANGHAI
The bib splitter under the Ferrari's chassis was new and concealed most of the ballast inside it. Instead of having an upside down L-section (see circle), it had two vertical end plates which, together with the shape of the central area, created a kind of venturi effect, able to better channel air towards the central part of the diffuser.

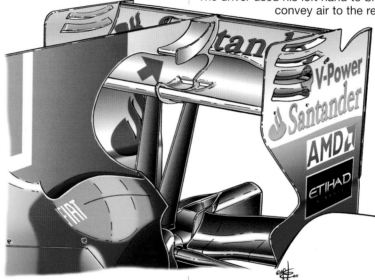

COCKPIT HOLE
The driver used his left hand to bring the blow system into play to convey air to the rear wing. The hole was at the side of the steering wheel, partially hidden by the deformable structure at the driver's side; he had a glove with special padding to make the manoeuvre easier.

BARCELLONA
Ferrari's active system made its debut in Spain. It was operated by only two "ears" at the sides of the engine cover. The illustration shows the channelling that conveyed air towards the cockpit when the hole was open, and towards the wing when the driver closed the hole on the straight. Also visible is the channelling that conducted air towards the lower part of the rear end.

ISTANBUL
As expected, Ferrari modified the means by which the driver operated the blow system towards the rear wing. When the control made its debut at Barcelona, the hole to be closed was inside the cockpit to the left of the steering wheel (see circle). A manoeuvre that was not so easy for Fernando Alonso, despite the fact that his steering wheel was closer to the hole. In Turkey, the interior tube was lengthened forwards, exploiting the space between the leg protection structure so that the system could be operated with the left foot. The rest of this complex arrangement remained the same.

MONACO
Ferrari was the only top team to exploit the opportunity of placing a small plane attached directly to the fin in the central 15 cm. Of course, Maranello did not take their F-duct to Monaco, which next appeared in Turkey.

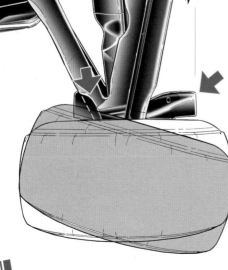

STEERING
At Monaco, the Ferrari's suspension arms were more robust, having been modified to provide a greater steering angle from 14° to 22°, which was useful going into the old Lowes corner.

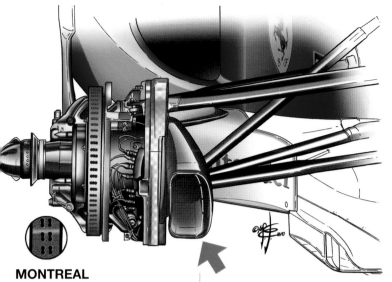

FRONT WING

There were low downforce wings for everyone, while Ferrari had modified the upper flap (1) with an internal reduced chord and they added a small vertical fin (2) in the central zone (1) of the main flap, which also had a reduced chord, all to improve the air flow towards the lower area of the car.

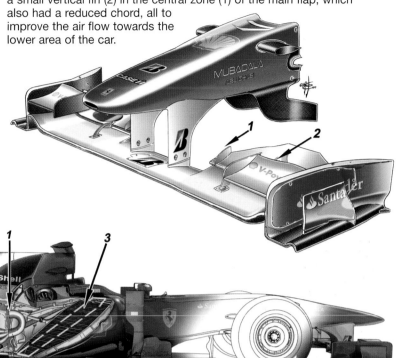

MONTREAL

All the teams took more powerful braking systems with bigger air intakes to Montreal. Ferrari's standard dimension braking system is shown in yellow.
It has become a sort of tradition for Maranello to use Carbon Industries discs in Canada, in place of the usual Brembo units.

VALENCIA

The most important stage in the development of the F 10 appeared at Valencia with the introduction of low exhausts and a concentration of modifications that went well beyond moving the exhaust blow from the high, advanced position (1) to the low and set back one (2). The disposition of the radiators (3) was new and they were slightly bigger and inclined; the body was also modified in the lower rear area.
And, of course, all the lower aerodynamics were revised to optimise the advantages obtained from the exhaust blow at the sides of the diffusers' lateral channels. Massa also had a new gearbox, which enabled the team to raise the suspension mounts.

EXHAUSTS

The F 10's exhausts exited from the lower part of the end of the sidepods (1) with a rounded terminal that was not cut like a "slice of salami", as on the Red Bull until the Grand Prix of Canada; at Valencia, the RB6 had a vertically cut terminal.
All the part above the exhausts had anti-heat plates (2) and adhesive thermal variants applied both to the modified diffusers and the suspension elements (3) as well as the end plates of the rear wing.
The engine detail clearly shows that the exhausts were no longer upside down and had a very low terminal area.

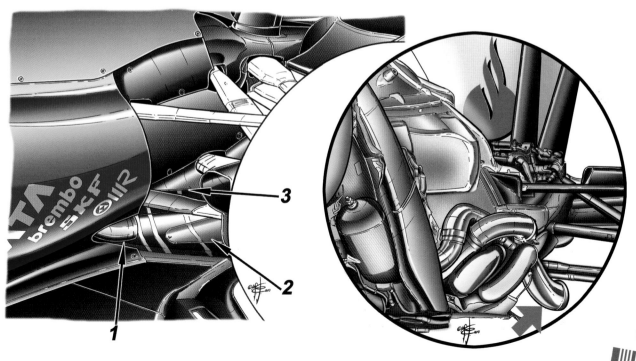

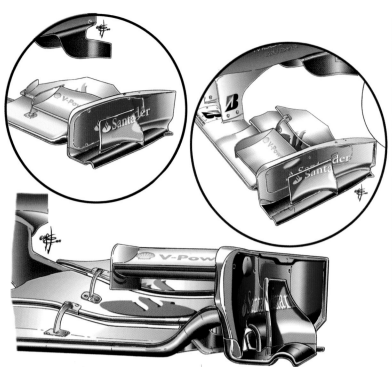

HOCKENHEIM

Here, there was further refinement of the Silverstone F 10's exhausts and diffusers; the illustration compares the Valencia system with the one used on the Friday, while on the Saturday a slightly longer version was installed.

Valencia

SILVERSTONE

For the first time during the 2010 season, Ferrari replaced their single flap (see circle above) with double, much curled element to achieve more downforce at the front end, being able to better exploit subsequent greater incidence of them both.

Note in the detail below the double tail fins in the lower area of the car – there was only one on the old car – and the vertical section of the end plate, which opened towards the outside down low.

Massa

Alonso

REAR WING

On the low downforce circuit of Spa, Massa used a new rear wing in qualifying and the race. It was easily recognisable by its new Red Bull-style end plates and the position of the gills in the upper area. The wing was also briefly seen in Canada, but it was not used in that country. It generated less load compared to the one on Alonso's F 10 in rain set-up.

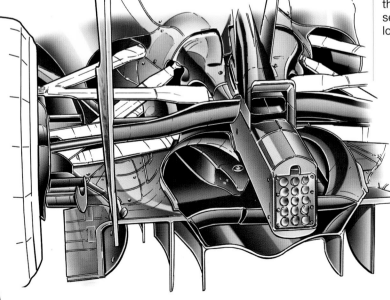

BUDAPEST

In detail, the modifications to the F 10's diffusers introduced in Germany. The flat part, at the sides of the wheels, became curved upwards at the leading edge and was the one most affected by the hot air flow from the exhausts. The walls of the lateral channels were also modified, becoming more inclined and protected by anti-heat material.

DIFFUSER

The F 10 taken to Belgium had a completely new rear end, due in part to the introduction of a new gearbox after its crash test in July, which had small gills to increase the volume of the double diffuser.

The unit had a "vortex" instead of a hole, following the path taken some time earlier by Renault and McLaren (see circle); there were also two longitudinal extensions in observance of the regulations.

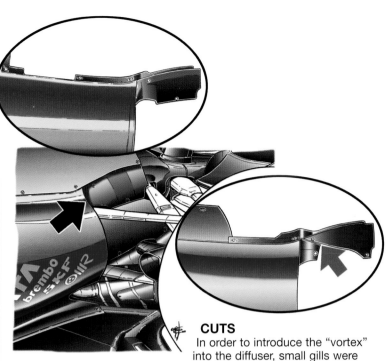

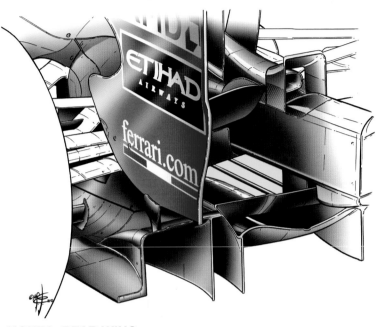

CUTS

In order to introduce the "vortex" into the diffuser, small gills were added to the body à la Renault and McLaren (see circle). These meant the regulations were respected as they stipulated that the sky should be seen when inspecting the double diffuser area from below.

The same gills were also applied to the new gearbox. In the illustration showing terminal part of the body one can see how, compared to the basic solution that came in at Valencia, they attained a new example (below in the oval) which respects the regulations due to the small cuts, even if carried out in a nit picking manner.

MONZA: REAR WING

On the Friday, the two drivers carried out comparative testing of two aerodynamic packages, although they were not too different from each other. At the rear end, the chosen proportions were extremely interesting, because as well as having planes (4) ad hoc (straight and with smaller chord) an F-duct conduit (1) was also included and was especially designed for a smaller flap with a different and small section.

The end plates had no gills (2) or little vertical Gurney flap (3).

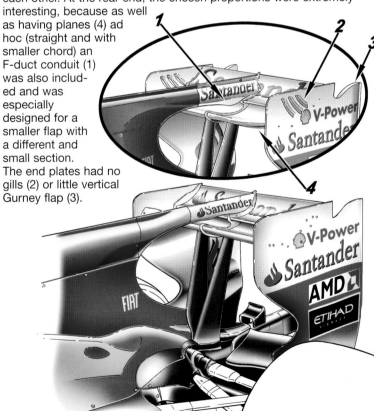

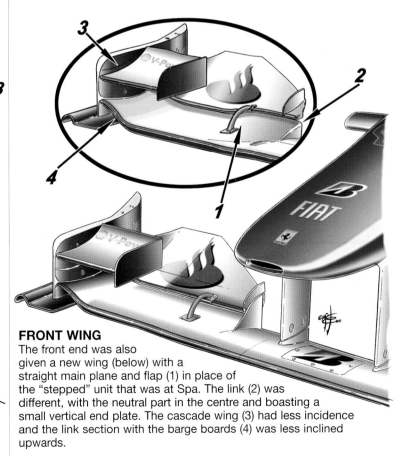

FRONT WING

The front end was also given a new wing (below) with a straight main plane and flap (1) in place of the "stepped" unit that was at Spa. The link (2) was different, with the neutral part in the centre and boasting a small vertical end plate. The cascade wing (3) had less incidence and the link section with the barge boards (4) was less inclined upwards.

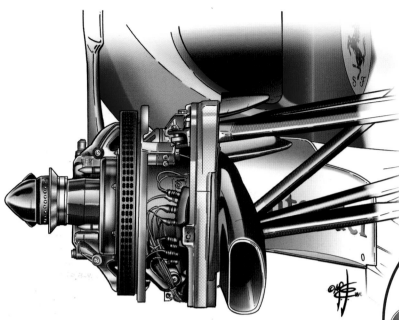

SINGAPORE: DISC BRAKES
Both Ferraris had new Brembo disc brakes at Singapore, with three holes in-line first seen at Monza and used only by Alonso in the GP of Italy. Those holes ensured better heat dissipation.

SINGAPORE
The knife edge zone under the chassis was also modified. It was the one suspected of being too flexible and subjected to a new and more severe crash test at the scrutineering headquarters from Monza onwards. The new version is in the oval.

FRONT WING
Alonso and Massa had three different front wings available to them and they tested them systematically on the Friday. The Spaniard concentrated on the two with double flaps, while Massa also tried the Monaco unit with its single flap. In the end, the choice was in favour of the new version, which differed from the one that debuted at Silverstone due to the regression of the small external end plate of about 8-10 cm.

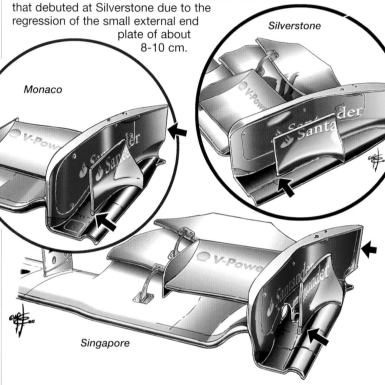

SUZUKA
In Japan, the F10 was given a new plane that provided more downforce. It was upside down omega shaped and was above the deformable structure (the old version is in the circle) which was also slightly modified and the zone inside the rear wheels was more curved.

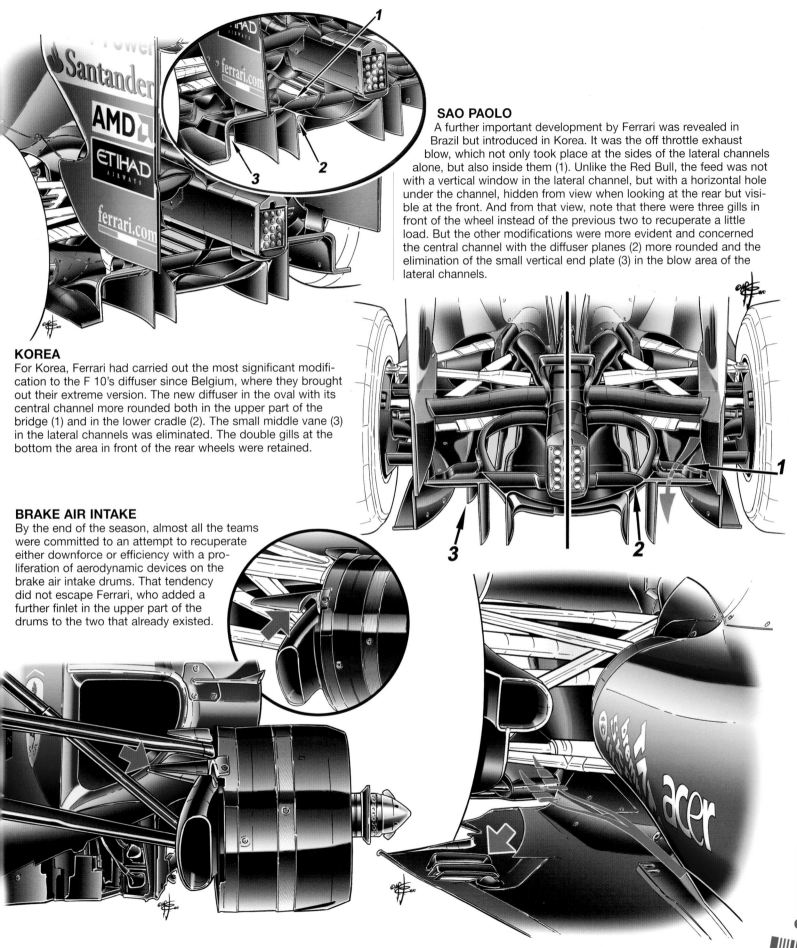

SAO PAOLO

A further important development by Ferrari was revealed in Brazil but introduced in Korea. It was the off throttle exhaust blow, which not only took place at the sides of the lateral channels alone, but also inside them (1). Unlike the Red Bull, the feed was not with a vertical window in the lateral channel, but with a horizontal hole under the channel, hidden from view when looking at the rear but visible at the front. And from that view, note that there were three gills in front of the wheel instead of the previous two to recuperate a little load. But the other modifications were more evident and concerned the central channel with the diffuser planes (2) more rounded and the elimination of the small vertical end plate (3) in the blow area of the lateral channels.

KOREA

For Korea, Ferrari had carried out the most significant modification to the F 10's diffuser since Belgium, where they brought out their extreme version. The new diffuser in the oval with its central channel more rounded both in the upper part of the bridge (1) and in the lower cradle (2). The small middle vane (3) in the lateral channels was eliminated. The double gills at the bottom the area in front of the rear wheels were retained.

BRAKE AIR INTAKE

By the end of the season, almost all the teams were committed to an attempt to recuperate either downforce or efficiency with a proliferation of aerodynamic devices on the brake air intake drums. That tendency did not escape Ferrari, who added a further finlet in the upper part of the drums to the two that already existed.

Monza *Singapore*

MONZA-SINGAPORE COMPARISON

One of the most exciting moments in Ferrari's technical comeback coincided with their two consecutive victories at Monza and in Singapore on two completely opposed circuits in terms of technical characteristics, especially as far as aerodynamic load is concerned, shown in both the frontal and three quarter views.

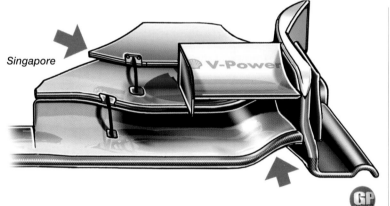

Singapore

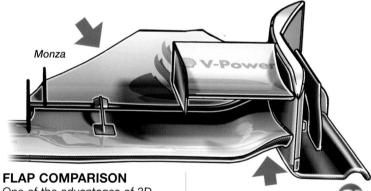

Monza

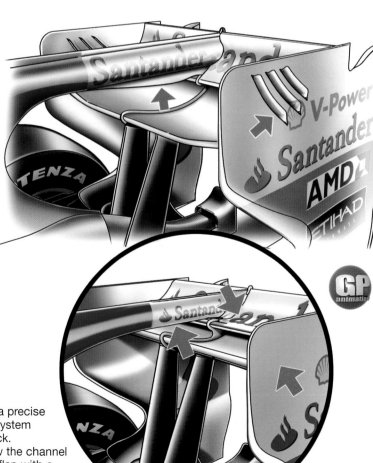

FLAP COMPARISON

One of the advantages of 3D animation is that it is possible to easily make a comparison of details in an identical position, as can be clearly seen in these frames, showing the double flap solution and the more raised plane of Singapore compared to the lower downforce single flap with a less curved plane.

MONZA F-DUCT

The Monza victory was partly due to a precise aerodynamic set-up, with an F-duct system specially developed for the Italian track. Compared to Spa, it can be seen how the channel is much smaller, having to work on a flap with a smaller chord.

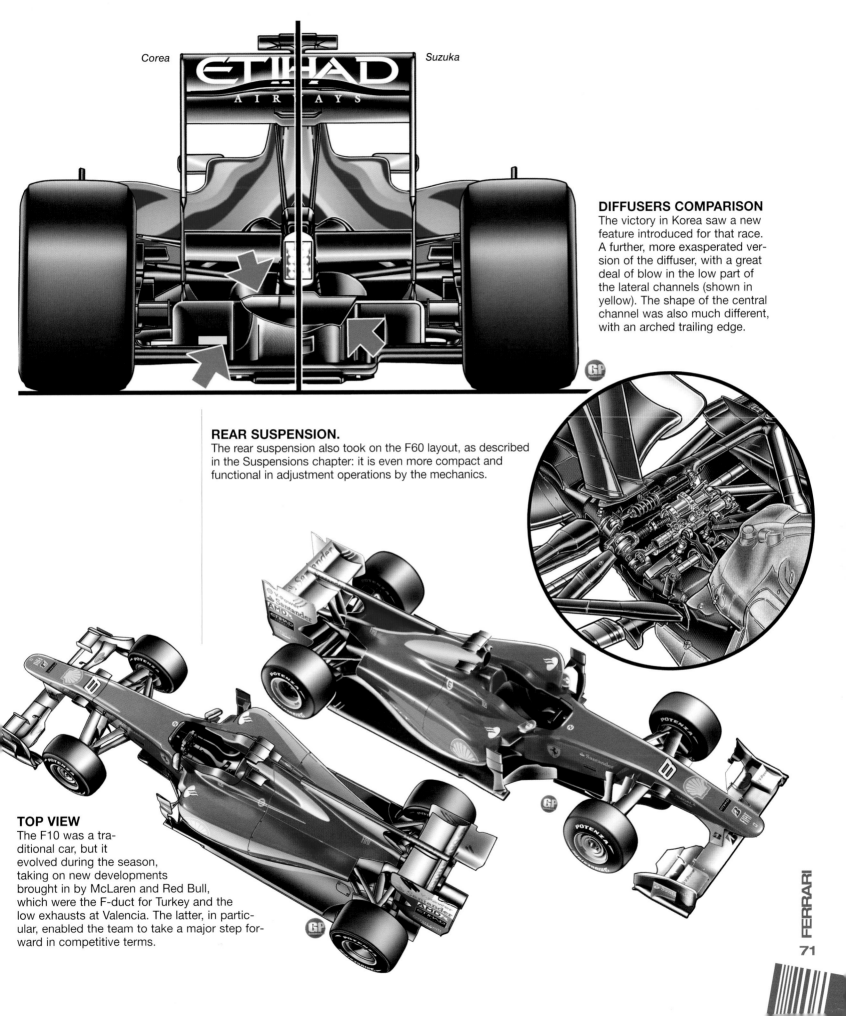

Corea

Suzuka

DIFFUSERS COMPARISON

The victory in Korea saw a new feature introduced for that race. A further, more exasperated version of the diffuser, with a great deal of blow in the low part of the lateral channels (shown in yellow). The shape of the central channel was also much different, with an arched trailing edge.

REAR SUSPENSION.

The rear suspension also took on the F60 layout, as described in the Suspensions chapter: it is even more compact and functional in adjustment operations by the mechanics.

TOP VIEW

The F10 was a traditional car, but it evolved during the season, taking on new developments brought in by McLaren and Red Bull, which were the F-duct for Turkey and the low exhausts at Valencia. The latter, in particular, enabled the team to take a major step forward in competitive terms.

COMPARISON OF CUT-AWAYS

The F10's architecture was derived from that of the F60, both in terms of chassis shape with the longer fuel tank area, and the disposition of the radiators. The position of the engine-gearbox group was new, as it was installed at a 3.5° angle.

UNDERBODY COMPARISON

The underbodies of the two cars were very different. In the end, Ferrari was the team that best interpreted the hot blow introduced by Red Bull, being able to also blow hot air under the lateral channels and not just above them, also interacting with the central one. Note in the view from below the space created for the double diffuser, with many small longitudinal devices in order to respect the regulations.

PLANE
Under the skin of a project that was an evolution of the F60, the Ferrari F10 hid a major new development: its engine inclined by 3.5° to provide more volume for the diffuser.

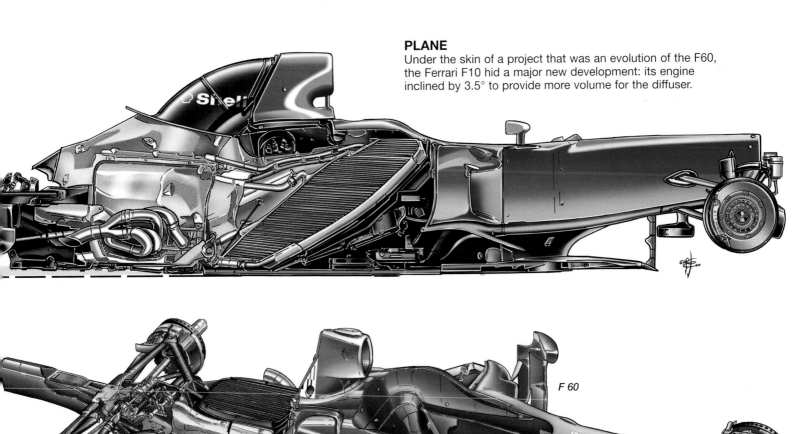

F 60

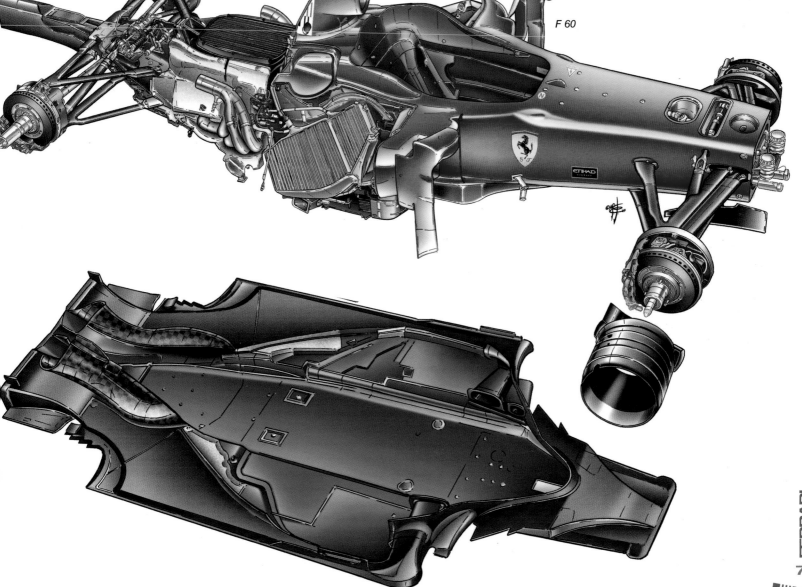

After having acquired Brawn GP, world champions with Jenson Button in 2009, the official debut of Mercedes-Benz in 2010 was decidedly negative.

The matter becomes even more so if one considers that this was the team that had introduced the double diffuser, which was liberalised for 2010, and should have meant Mercedes could count on greater experience in that area. Instead, the MGP W01 disappointed in exploiting that self-same development.

Despite the substantial increase in fuel tank volume, the team kept its car's wheelbase more or less the same as last year – it was just 2 cm longer, compared to the McLaren's 26 cm increase – Mercedes were forced to design an extremely short gearbox, as a result of which it limited development potential in the double diffuser zone.

A problem that could not be resolved even when it was discovered, because it would have required the construction of a new transmission.

The fact is that Brawn GP had enjoyed a notable temporary advantage in the design stage, but more than anything else it was created with a budget that was not so limited after Honda had retired from F1.

The design of the new Mercedes-Benz was started before the Germans bought the team, at a time when the company had lost many talented people – the first Jorge Zender – and had just about finished its budget, so it reduced the number of personnel in its technical and other offices.

At its launch, the MGP W01 invited curiosity due to the shape of its roll bar, which had become like a blade with the engine air intake built around it like a simple piece of the bodywork.

A feature that left space for future developments, which then materialised at the Grand Prix of Spain, where a very low engine cover was introduced with the air intake comprising two small ears at the sides of the roll bar's pyramid. An interesting aspect, because it enabled the team to notably reduce the section of the car in the central area to the advantage of clean air flowing towards the rear wing.

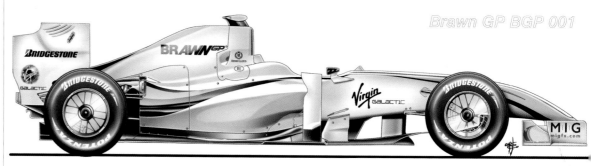
Brawn GP BGP 001

Mercedes MGP W01

Mercedes MGP W01
Test

Mercedes MGP W01
Baharain

Mercedes MGP W01
Shanghai

But it was a solution that created doubt about safety if the car turned over on soft or sandy ground. The pyramid shaped roll bar became a boomerang when the team decided it had to follow McLaren's F-duct technique.

In fact, it did not permit the creation of a fin-like engine cover so as not to lose advantages in terms of penetration of the two small air intake ears.

MERCEDES

CONSTRUCTORS' CLASSIFICATION		
	2009	2010
Position	2°(Brawn)	4°

Mercedes MGP W01
Barcelona

Mercedes MGP W01
Valencia

Mercedes MGP W01
Monza

Mercedes MGP W01
Singapore

After that, Mercedes-Benz opted for a highly laborious F-duct with the air pipes flowing through the front part of the chassis and the rear wing, which travelled through extremely narrow channels inside the diffuser and the end plates. It was an expensive business, among other things, and limited the development of the diffusers in the second part of the season. The exhaust blow, the same as that of Red Bull, was introduced at Valencia but required more diffuser development, which was made difficult again by their internal channelling. The only positive note was the extreme ease of the F-duct's operation with the left foot. From the outset, the MPG W01 suffered from chronic understeer, which the team tried to remedy for the Grand Prix of Spain. They lengthened the wheelbase, inclining the front suspension wishbones and the wing supports forward without having to redesign the nose, which would have required a crash test. Then weight distribution was modified, with more load on the back end.

But when it is all boiled down, fourth place in the world championship rewarded the "young" team's recovery efforts, as it was able to place itself immediately behind the three great protagonists of the season even though they were never able to fight for a single victory.

TOP VIEW

Seen from above, one can also note how the Mercedes-Benz was the car with the shortest wheelbase, as well as the contained length of the sidepods as on the 2009 Brawn. The rounded shapes and the characteristic single flap at the front end remained. But note the Red Bull influence in the protrusion of the initial part of the chassis.

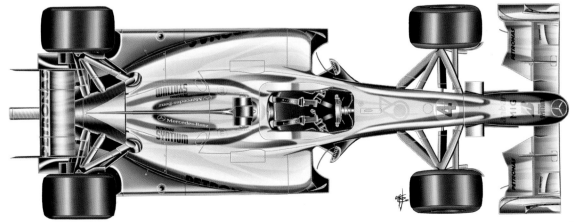

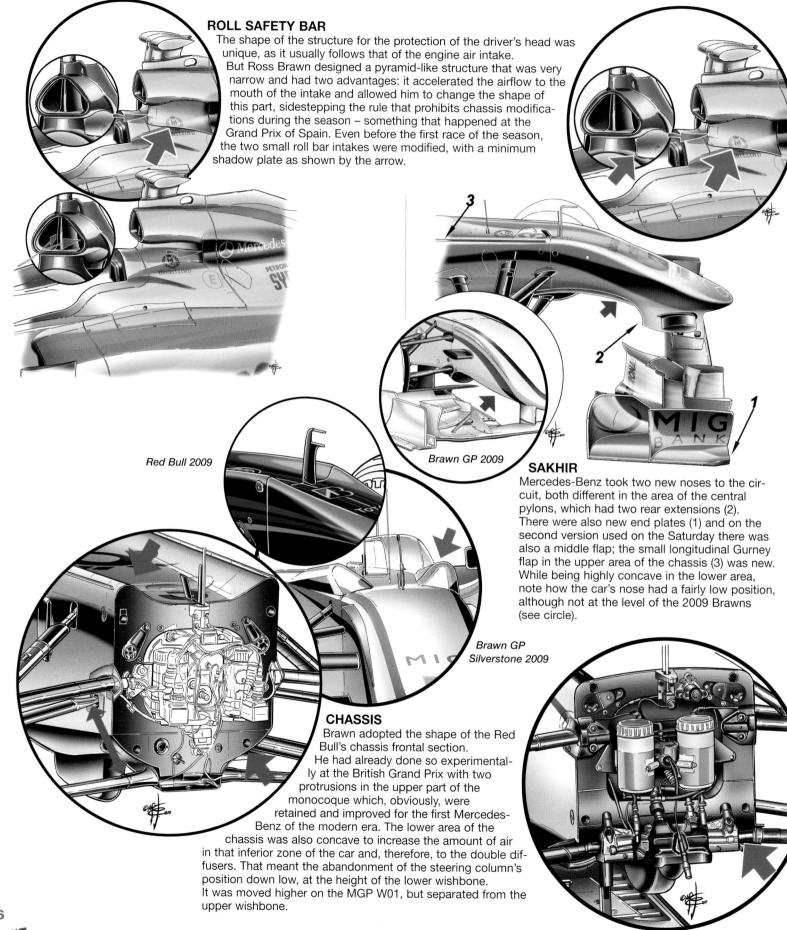

ROLL SAFETY BAR

The shape of the structure for the protection of the driver's head was unique, as it usually follows that of the engine air intake. But Ross Brawn designed a pyramid-like structure that was very narrow and had two advantages: it accelerated the airflow to the mouth of the intake and allowed him to change the shape of this part, sidestepping the rule that prohibits chassis modifications during the season – something that happened at the Grand Prix of Spain. Even before the first race of the season, the two small roll bar intakes were modified, with a minimum shadow plate as shown by the arrow.

Red Bull 2009

Brawn GP 2009

SAKHIR

Mercedes-Benz took two new noses to the circuit, both different in the area of the central pylons, which had two rear extensions (2). There were also new end plates (1) and on the second version used on the Saturday there was also a middle flap; the small longitudinal Gurney flap in the upper area of the chassis (3) was new. While being highly concave in the lower area, note how the car's nose had a fairly low position, although not at the level of the 2009 Brawns (see circle).

Brawn GP
Silverstone 2009

CHASSIS

Brawn adopted the shape of the Red Bull's chassis frontal section. He had already done so experimentally at the British Grand Prix with two protrusions in the upper part of the monocoque which, obviously, were retained and improved for the first Mercedes-Benz of the modern era. The lower area of the chassis was also concave to increase the amount of air in that inferior zone of the car and, therefore, to the double diffusers. That meant the abandonment of the steering column's position down low, at the height of the lower wishbone. It was moved higher on the MGP W01, but separated from the upper wishbone.

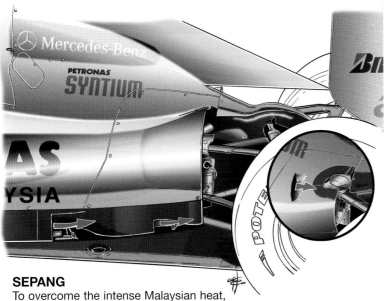

SEPANG

To overcome the intense Malaysian heat, the exhaust area was covered with a part of the bodywork that looked like a loudhailer, to better expel hot air towards the rear. The previous version seen in Melbourne is in the circle and has a Ferrari-style gill connected, as always, by a narrow slot to respect the single exhaust opening regulation.

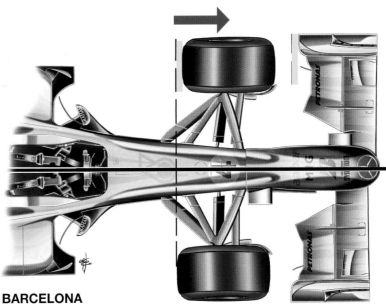

BARCELONA

Mercedes-Benz lengthened its car's wheelbase for the Grand Prix of Spain, distancing the front axle from the body to obtain three results: weight moved to the rear end to improve traction, make the car less nervous and more suited to Michael Schumacher's driving style; improve the aerodynamics by distancing the turbulence created by the front tyres that affected the car's body. The front suspension wishbones were inclined forward by 50 mm and the front wing moved up, revising the support pillars, which were also inclined forward, as can be seen in the illustration showing the front wing detail. The short wheelbase car was used once more, this time at the subsequent Grand Prix of Monaco.

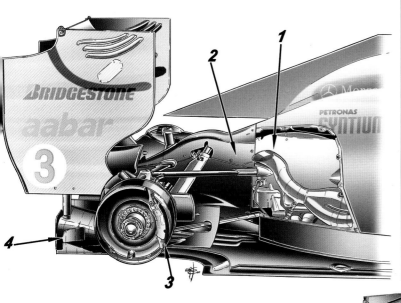

REAR END COMPARISON

Mercedes-Benz retained its high exhausts (1) as on the previous Brawn GP car for the first part of the season, with the exit shooting hot air up high. 2) The internal fairing, which wrapped itself around all the mechanics and gearbox, was very clean. The main difference comprised the position of the brake calipers (3); they were no longer prone to free space in the lateral channels zone of the double diffuser, which had small fins (4) to better direct the air to that zone.

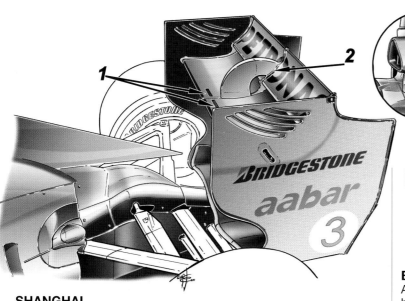

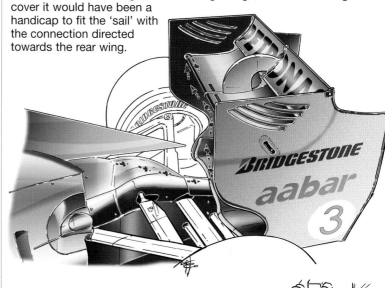

SHANGHAI

In China, Mercedes-Benz introduced its passive F-duct system, which did not have to be operated by the driver. It had two small air entry intakes and this voluminous lung, which blew directly into the flap that had a slot at the rear.

BARCELONA

At the Grand Prix of Spain, it became clear why the Mercedes-Benz had been designed with a pyramid-like structure in the area of the roll bar. At the sides of the knife edge protection structural zone, small low air intakes appeared to reduce the section in this area, all to the advantage of the flow of clean air to the rear wing. The two previous versions are shown in the circles. It was not considered necessary to adopt the F-duct during the car's design stage, but with this engine cover it would have been a handicap to fit the 'sail' with the connection directed towards the rear wing.

ISTANBUL

The management of air flow by the Mercedes-Benz drivers was completely new. Ross Brawn had not wanted to thwart the advantage of the new knife edge engine cover, so he did not fit the conductors near the rear wing, as had McLaren previously, followed by many others. The air was gathered at the front end by two small intakes at the sides of the chassis in the area of the suspension mounts and, with a highly laborious but ingenious system, it interfered with the blow into the main plane of the wing, passing from the diffusers and the end plates, which were concave on the inside to contain a narrow channel. This technical complication also damaged the development of the diffusers in relation to the team's adversaries.

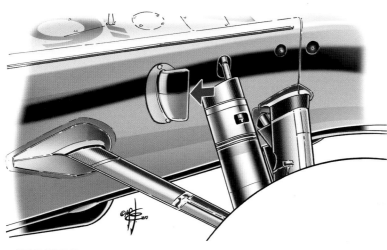

VALENCIA

The debut of the low exhausts at Valencia was not very positive, their format similar to that of Ferrari. The illustration clearly shows the new progression of the exhaust collectors, which blew downwards. The completely closed off terminal part of the body created some overheating problems.

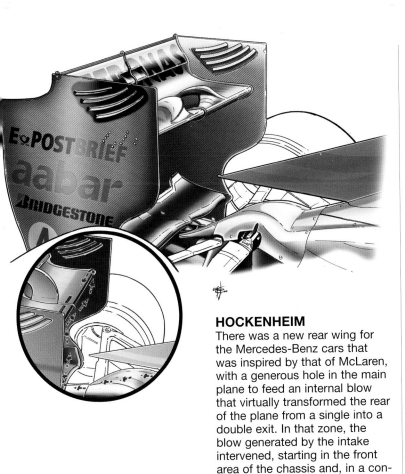

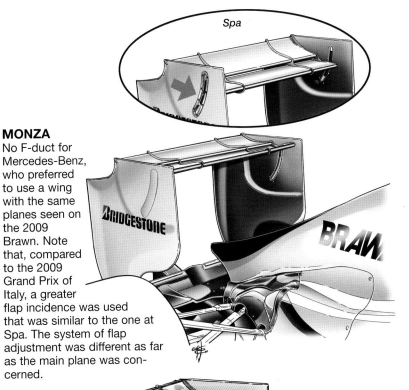

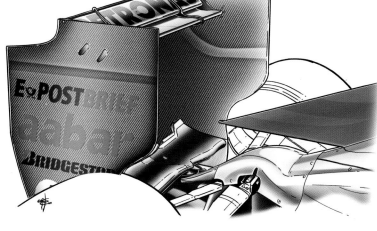

MONZA
No F-duct for Mercedes-Benz, who preferred to use a wing with the same planes seen on the 2009 Brawn. Note that, compared to the 2009 Grand Prix of Italy, a greater flap incidence was used that was similar to the one at Spa. The system of flap adjustment was different as far as the main plane was concerned.

HOCKENHEIM
There was a new rear wing for the Mercedes-Benz cars that was inspired by that of McLaren, with a generous hole in the main plane to feed an internal blow that virtually transformed the rear of the plane from a single into a double exit. In that zone, the blow generated by the intake intervened, starting in the front area of the chassis and, in a contorted sort of way, went through the inside of the end plates as shown in detail in the circle.

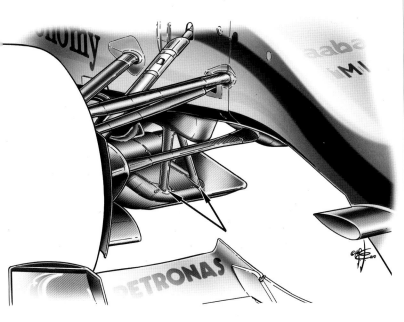

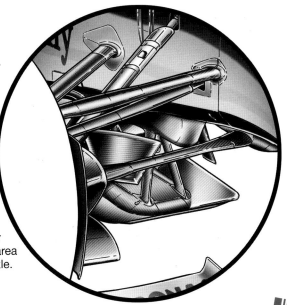

SINGAPORE
The final modification for 2010, with work already concentrated on the 2011 car. That is the way they used these upside down-V barge boards, located in the lower area of the chassis to improve the management of the air flow in the lower area above the front axle.

T-TRAY
A new and more severe test of the t-tray under the chassis went into effect at Monza, a move suggested by Ross Brawn and McLaren; strangely, the only team to carry out the modification was Mercedes-Benz; a doubling of elements with two upside down V-fixings.

The post-Pat Symonds 2010 season was a difficult one for Renault, with James Allison promoted to technical director of the team. Problems with the wind tunnel, which was to have been given an important moving ground upgrade, did the rest despite the strengthening of the CFD department.

The new R30 was conceived before the improvements arrived and the car suffered badly on the track when it came up against the top teams in the early races. There was a family air about the new car, which was similar to the old R29, especially the nose, which had simply been slimmed down slightly but it was considerably lower and voluminous compared to those of its opponents. But all the other configurations they tried were less effective in air flow management in the lower part of the car.

The longitudinal stiffening arm remained between the gearbox and the monocoque and has been a feature of all the Renaults in F1 since it was introduced with the V-111° engine, which obviously required that kind of rigidity, way back in 2001.

With the R30, this device was even more useful because they built a decidedly long gearbox to achieve the considerable volume of the double diffuser.

While the blow into the diffusers arrived fairly early – at the GP of Valencia, like Ferrari – and as with Maranello it immediately worked properly, the F-duct was extremely late being used on the track and was laborious to operate. In theory, it was programmed for use at Silverstone,

Renault R29

Renault R30

Renault R30
Test

Renault R30
Sepang

Renault R30
Barcelona

Renault R30
Montreal

CONSTRUCTORS' CLASSIFICATION		
	2009	2010
Position	8°	5°

Renault R30
Valencia

Renault R30
Budapest

Renault R30
Spa

Renault R30
Monza

Renault R30
Abu Dahbi

but it did not arrive until Spa. When it did, though, it became an immediate step forward in performance terms.

Alonso learnt that to his disadvantage as he chased the mirage of the world championship in the closing race at Abu Dhabi; due to the F-duct on his Renault, Petrov was able to deny the Spaniard the fourth place he needed to win the world championship.

It should be noted that from its introduction the exhaust blow took place with the use of retarded ignition, originally developed for Red Bull.

Renault carried out a great deal of development work, especially on the front wing with more or less an ad hoc solution for every Grand Prix. No fewer than seven evolutions of the diffusers were used. And apart from continuous aerodynamic refinements, the team worked on two sectors of the car in particular due to pressure from the drivers: they were the braking system and the power steering. The former to make it more powerful and rigid by the adoption, in two different moments, of Brembo calipers instead of those of A+P.

Kubica's car was fitted with them in Canada by way of a test, so that both cars used the Italian calipers from Valencia.

Both drivers had complained about the heaviness of the power steering in the early part of the season.

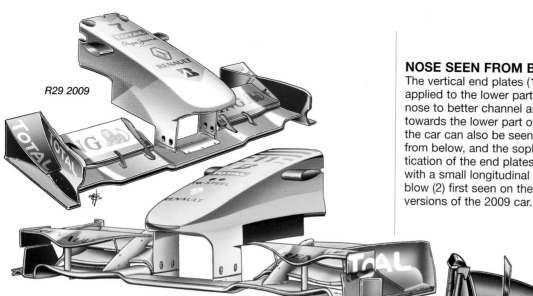

R29 2009

NOSE SEEN FROM BELOW

The vertical end plates (1) applied to the lower part of the nose to better channel air towards the lower part of the car can also be seen from below, and the sophistication of the end plates with a small longitudinal blow (2) first seen on the later versions of the 2009 car.

R29 2009

NOSE

All the elements were completely new, but the Renault nose did partially retain the abundant and square dimensions of the 2009 car. The two vertical end plates remained and were applied at the sides, even if they were less voluminous. Note the much spooned flap in the central area and the end plates with three separate elements, which were much more evolved than those on the R29 at the start of the season.

MELBOURNE

Renault went to almost every GP with more refined noses, so here we have grouped the most significant of them together.

The second evolution appeared in Australia after the one first seen in Bahrain: the changes were concentrated on the small end plates applied to the cascade wing, which was still highly spooned, and had become even smaller, with a wing plane shape instead of square (see circle).

VALENCIA-SILVERSTONE

The Renault front wing evolution continued. In the illustration, we see the Silverstone unit compared to the one used in Valencia (see circle). The modifications mainly concern the end plates. Two small flaps were added, one at the start of the end plate – the previous raised flap had been eliminated – and one at the end. The objective was, as always, to optimise the air flow around the front wheels.

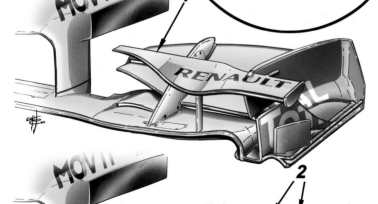

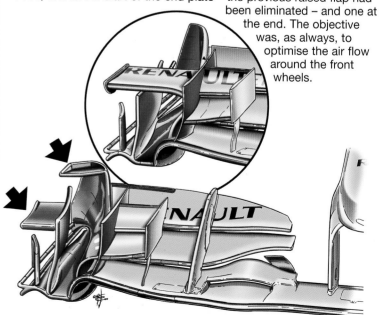

MONTREAL

A front wing of medium-low load was taken to Canada (below), without the cascade wing (1) and end plates cut and split (2). The height (1) of the small external fin was also different. But the comparison shows how the main plane was unchanged.

MONZA

The introduction of a new front wing was inevitable for the ultra-fast Monza circuit. Renault eliminated the parts of the vertical end plates and cascade wing that were on the car up to Spa (see circle). The V-cut in the flap was odd; its task was to create vortices able to energise the air flow in the car's central area.

SINGAPORE

The umpteenth Renault front wing appeared here, but without the T-element of the external end plate. In its place was a linked and rounded device that was to reduce the vortices, ensuring better consistency of yield. But the wing was only used by Kubica.

BRAKE AIR INTAKES

The R30's brake air intakes became increasingly effective aerodynamic devices. These curved double fins applied at the limits of the internal barge boards, set a trend during the season.

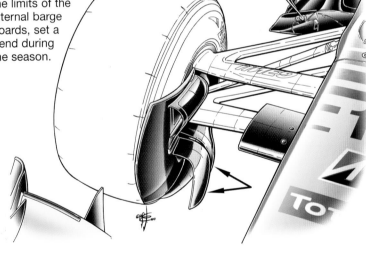

TURNING VANES

Two highly twisted turning vanes were also on the car, combined with features adopted for the nose and in relation to a sort of mini-skirt in the lower area of the chassis.
The illustration refers to the GP of Canada, where Brembo calipers were tested for the first time in place of those of A+P. The Brembo units later became those used by both cars from the subsequent Valencia GP.

MONTREAL

Renault gets the credit for designing the most innovative wing fielded at the medium-low downforce circuit in Montreal. The V-shape of the main plane is unusual and was to reduce resistance on the straight.

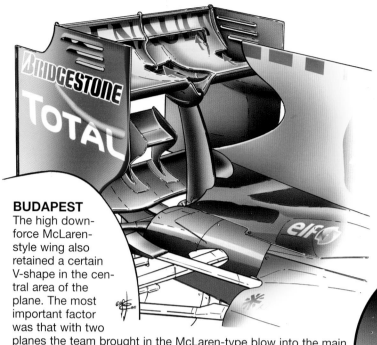

BUDAPEST

The high down-force McLaren-style wing also retained a certain V-shape in the central area of the plane. The most important factor was that with two planes the team brought in the McLaren-type blow into the main unit. That was done in an extremely complicated manner, with a large hole in the plane and two laterals that integrated themselves with the flap, which also had blow as indicated by the arrows. The wing was first used by Kubica and then by Petrov.

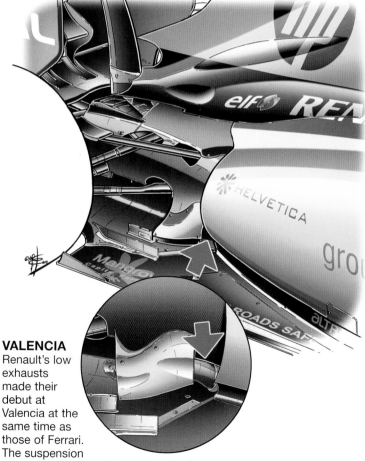

VALENCIA

Renault's low exhausts made their debut at Valencia at the same time as those of Ferrari. The suspension mounts were also raised. The exhaust exits had a sort of fairing to better direct the air flow towards to the sides of the lateral channels at the rear of the car and, partially, underneath them.

R29
2009

DIFFUSER

The hole in the central area of the diffuser was practically a "vortex" using a technique that was seen in the last pre-season test session on the McLaren. The French company brought forward the official debut of the hole to the Grand Prix of Malaysia; it can be easily seen in the view with the bottom disengaged, showing that it started much further forward compared to those of the other teams, and was much wider.

To adopt such a size and respect the regulations, two longitudinal fins (1) were applied and they also performed an aerodynamic function.

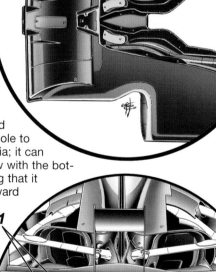

At the side we can see how simple and linear the 2009 Renault underbody was without the double diffuser. Note the absence of the central part of the underbody, while the majority of the teams used a technique in which the lower part of the chassis was also covered.

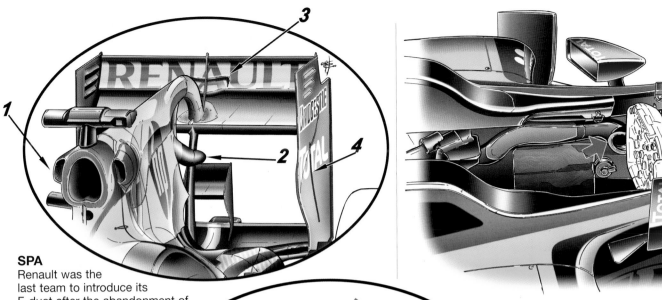

SPA

Renault was the last team to introduce its F-duct after the abandonment of the mildly effective initial project. But the Spa debut was extremely positive, even if it was a blend of features seen on other cars. As with the Ferrari, the Renault had two "ears" (1) at the sides of the engine air intake to feed the blow, a low air vent (2) as on the Red Bull, and the blow on the principal plane à la Force India and Mercedes-Benz. All of that combined with a blow flap (3) in the central area and sinuous end plates that had a small, vertical Gurney flap.

MONZA

For the ultra-fast Monza circuit, Renault simply used their Spa wing, with the trailing edge of the flap boasting a 3-4 cm cut.

F-DUCT HOLE

The management of the Renault F-duct also took place through a hole that was blocked off by the driver's left hand. It was a method that often created moments of panic: in an attempt to make up for the slight delay of the resistance reduction effect on the straight, the driver took his left hand away from the steering wheel in situations that were sometimes dangerous. – but the Renault F-duct immediately became one of the most efficient.

REAR SUSPENSION

To ensure diffusers of notable volume, the Renault R30's front suspension arms were heavily inclined forward.
Also note the much inclined link and the aerodynamic devices applied to the brake air intakes. The lower wishbone was slightly raised with the introduction of the blown exhausts.

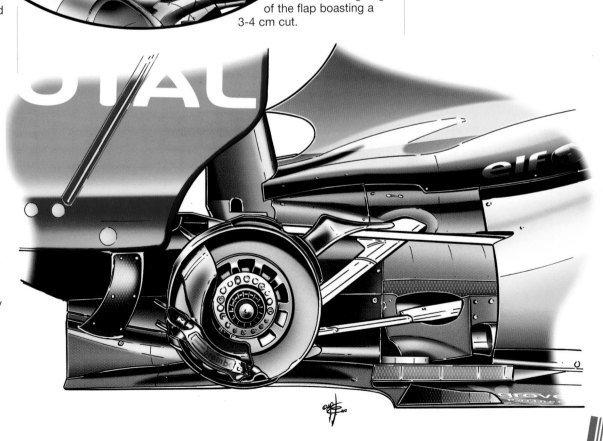

The team had a fairly positive 2009, when they climbed from eighth in the constructors' world championship table to sixth, scoring their first pole position in five years with the young Hulkenberg in Brazil. The advantage of using the double diffuser was partially thwarted by the difficulty of having to change engines.

After three years of using the 8-cylinder Toyota, along came the new 8-cylinder Cosworth after the Japanese company's retirement. To all the normal complications of having to install a new power unit was added the lack of precise reference data, given that the legendary British firm had not competed in F1 since 2006.

It was actually the 2006 unit that was the basis from which the design of the new 2010 engine began, without being able to conduct a real shakedown on the track. The notable and ambitious evolution of the exhausts blowing directly into the central channel, originally designed in October for the Toyota V 8, was later replaced by the safer solution with exhausts that exited from the upper areas of the sidepods. The same evolution introduced by Red Bull with the exhausts in the lower part of the 'pods were implemented by Williams with a slight delay. The team had other priorities, like consolidating the reliability of the engine and increasing its power output.

Without reference data, the study of fuel tank capacity was more complicated than for other teams, even if at the end of the Grand Prix of Canada – the most demanding race of the season as far as fuel consumption goes – just 0.5 kg of fuel was left in the tank, a sign that the team had achieved its objective.

The FW31's wheelbase increase was contained, partially due to an extremely short gearbox with a different position for the clutch, which was moved from the end of the engine to the 'box.

Right from its debut the FW32 project was a turnaround, especially in its front aerodynamics, with the introduction of a high nose and an extremely sophisticated wing group, which was the subject of continuous development during the season.

Compared to the 2009 car, not only can the higher nose be

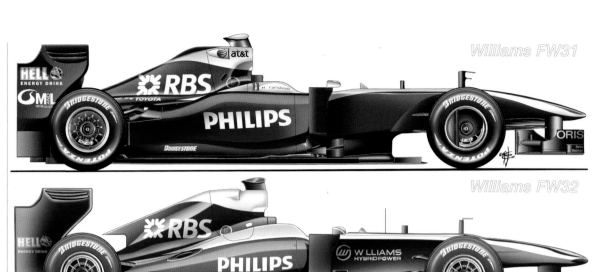

Williams FW31

Williams FW32

Williams FW32
Sakhir

Williams FW32
Barcelona

Williams FW32
Monaco

clearly seen but so can the disappearance of the deflectors in the lower area, replaced by a unit of the Brawn school with the knife edge zone under the chassis T-tray.

Sam Michael freely admitted that Williams had never previously thought of the F Duct feature, which came in as an experiment in China and then became a permanent fixture in Spain.

At the Catalonia circuit, the

arrangement had a completely different system in the way it was operated by the driver, and that is described in detail in the chapter on this new development.

The second feature that set a trend in 2010 was the low exhausts that blew into the lateral channels of the diffuser, but they did not make their debut until the Grand Prix of Great Britain for fear of the whole rear end burning. That was a very

costly programme, because they had to use a special material produced by one single company in France called Pyrossic to thermally insulate the lateral channels of the diffuser. Result: the first set of diffusers and the end of the engine cover cost a huge €25,000 each!

Later, in part due to the targeted use of this material in only the crucial points, the cost was substantially reduced. The exhausts

CONSTRUCTORS' CLASSIFICATION		
	2009	2010
Position	8°	6°

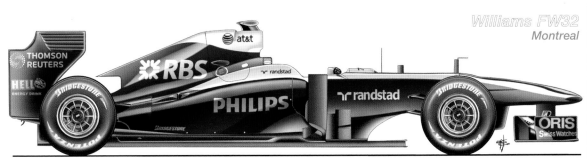

Williams FW32
Montreal

Williams FW32
Silverstone

Williams FW32
Monza

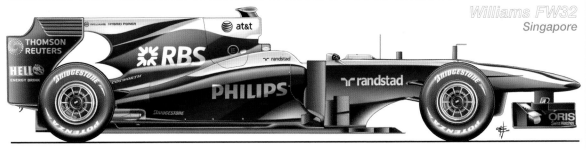

Williams FW32
Singapore

meant remaking the diffuser's lateral channels in two phases: the first appeared at Silverstone and the second at Hockenheim, while the engine blow, which was also being released, did not appear until Spa. As far as development during the season was concerned, the most significant stages came about at Barcelona with the debut of the F Duct, at Montreal, which saw new aerodynamics, but more than anything else with the different philosophy of correlation between mechani-

cal and aerodynamic set-ups suggested by Barrichello at Silverstone with low exhaust gills. The final advance came at Suzuka with new brake air intakes at the front and rear, a sector in which Williams distinguished itself both for the number of different solutions and their level of sophistication. The development of the season is described with a detailed reconstruction race-by-race, obviously with the help of Williams team.

A SEASON OF DEVELOPMENTS, RACE-BY-RACE:

Sakhir: two rear wings, RO4 (principal plane blown) and RO5, plus new Mk4 brake air intakes.
Melbourne: the same features.
Sepang: new DO3 diffuser with altered sections of serrated trim inside the tyres.
Bigger new intake 3206 for front brake cooling.
Shanghai: new front wing FO3 with new end plates and cascade wing. The F Duct with new RO8

rear wing was only tested on the Friday.
Barcelona: new aerodynamic package with an FO4 front wing, new in all its components; the F Duct also used in the race with the R11 wing – derived from the RO8 – and a new DO3 diffuser with modified central channel.
Monaco: new rear wing R3202 with a central hole of the main plane, but also of the beam wing (unique solution for 2010).
Istanbul: R12 low load rear wing and new rear brake air intake.
Montreal: two rear wings R14 and R15 to ensure two different levels of load and, obviously, a new front wing (F06), with totally different components. Front brake air intakes (3207 Mk 6b) and rears (3205 Mk4), which were considerably larger.
The bib splitter under the chassis was also replaced by two vertical tail fins under the nose.
Valencia: third evolution of the F Duct, combined with a new rear wing.
Silverstone: introduction of the exhaust blow combined with the new DO5 diffuser and two different engine covers, with and without a central blow in the terminal area. The brake air intake was modified by adding a further flap.
Hockenheim: further modification of the DO7 diffuser to better exploit the exhaust blow (update of the other tunnel, which works directly with exhaust gasses) Bib floor 3206 was also modified, as was the rear brake air intake again. New front wing F 09 with greater load.
Budapest: : the same aerodynamic configuration as the one used at Monaco.
Spa-Francorchamps: new F08 front wing of low-medium load, with a new curled third flap, combined with an equivalent new R21 rear wing with a reduced chord.
Monza: new R22 wing of low load for the rear end, made just for Monza, combined with the F Duct.
Singapore: the last aerodynamic package of the season with a new F10 front wing, revised in all

its elements and a D10 diffuser considerably modified in the central channel (enlarged) and modification 3207 to the bib floor. New 3206 sidepods, combined with no fewer than three different engine covers: without central blow channel (3216), medium blow (3211), substantial blow (3214). In addition, blow exits at the sides of the cockpit (3202) became available, as did louvers (3201) in the low area and near the exhausts (3202) and the exhaust exit was modified (3213B).

Suzuka: the last development of the season appeared in Japan with new 3208 front brake air intakes with an enhanced Force India-like aerodynamic function plus rears (3207).

In summary, during the 2010 season, cars were entered for the 19 GPs with: nine different front wings, eight rears wings, seven diffusers, six engine covers, four front brake air intakes and six rears.

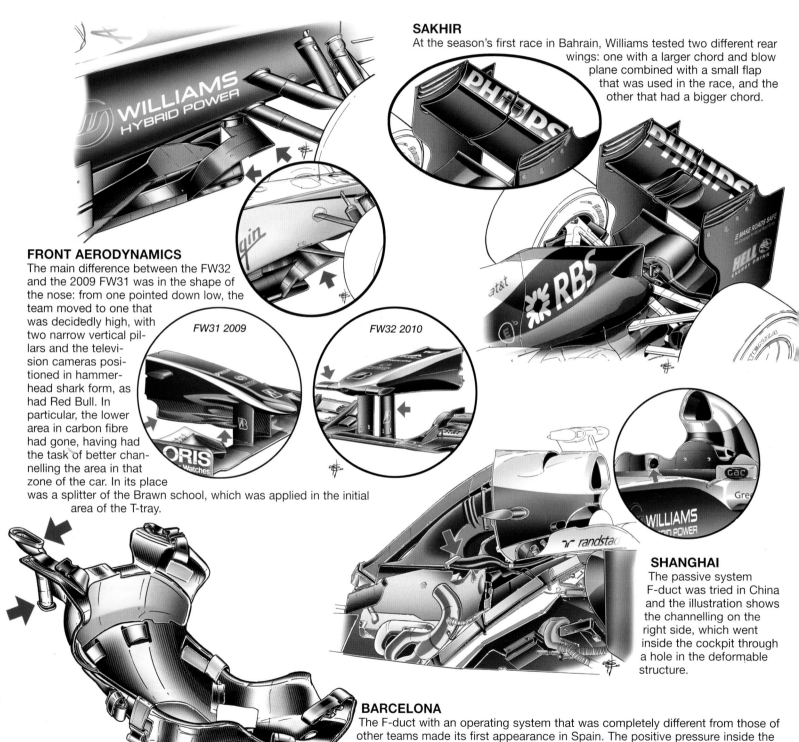

SAKHIR
At the season's first race in Bahrain, Williams tested two different rear wings: one with a larger chord and blow plane combined with a small flap that was used in the race, and the other that had a bigger chord.

FRONT AERODYNAMICS
The main difference between the FW32 and the 2009 FW31 was in the shape of the nose: from one pointed down low, the team moved to one that was decidedly high, with two narrow vertical pillars and the television cameras positioned in hammer-head shark form, as had Red Bull. In particular, the lower area in carbon fibre had gone, having had the task of better channelling the area in that zone of the car. In its place was a splitter of the Brawn school, which was applied in the initial area of the T-tray.

FW31 2009

FW32 2010

SHANGHAI
The passive system F-duct was tried in China and the illustration shows the channelling on the right side, which went inside the cockpit through a hole in the deformable structure.

BARCELONA
The F-duct with an operating system that was completely different from those of other teams made its first appearance in Spain. The positive pressure inside the cockpit was used and it was the driver's left leg that actioned the stall device of the rear wing through a hole in the seat. This will be explained in detail in the chapter on the F-duct.

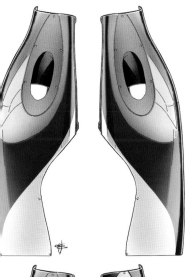

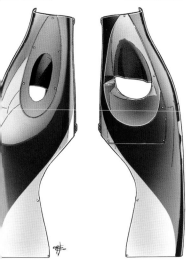

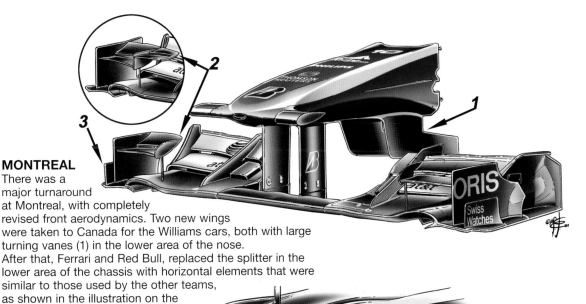

MONTREAL

There was a major turnaround at Montreal, with completely revised front aerodynamics. Two new wings were taken to Canada for the Williams cars, both with large turning vanes (1) in the lower area of the nose. After that, Ferrari and Red Bull, replaced the splitter in the lower area of the chassis with horizontal elements that were similar to those used by the other teams, as shown in the illustration on the right/left. The second version of the front wing is shown in the circle, with its cascade wing that has an extension (2) with a slight negative lift. The outsides of the end plates were also different (3). This new example was used in the race.

ENGINE COVERS

During the season, Williams used no fewer than six different engine covers, but these three, viewed from the top, had fundamentally different shapes. The first is the example used at the beginning of the season, which was symmetrical for tracks that did not require substantial thermal dissipation; the second was for hot Grands Prix that came in at Sepang, while the third shows the comparison with the new engine cover (right) combined at Silverstone with low exhausts.

MONACO

High load wings for Monaco, with the blow system in the principal plane introduced the previous year by McLaren and used by many of the teams in the 2010 season. In fact, the blow transformed the rear wing group into a tri-plane with two trailing edges of the main plane: the new feature was the use of the blow to the low plane above the deformable structure and that remained the only example to be used throughout the season. This design was also taken to other circuits to reduce in the incidence of the upper planes.

SILVERSTONE

Here, the low exhausts made their debut on the Friday morning at the start of practice, but only on Hulkenberg's car, together with a new engine cover/sidepods to make a direct comparison with the traditional solution mounted on the Barrichello car.

The latter was immediately successful and was fitted to both FW32s and retained for the race together with the new rear aerodynamics.

CUTS

This illustration shows just how much the text of the regulations quibble. To be able to widen the double underbody in the lower area of the car, you had to be able to see the sky when looking from down low. Cuts in the body work of all the cars appeared and looked ridiculous, their sole purpose respecting the letter of the letter of the regulations and, in correspondence, to be able to open the lower part to create the double diffusers.

HOCKENHEIM

Second development of the new diffuser created together with the low blow of the exhausts. In the circle (in both the detailed illustration and that of the complete diffuser) is the old, semi-triangular version, while the new one
in the illustration shows a bigger, squarer section at the leading edge, curved upwards. Only Barrichello had the new version in Germany, but it was on both cars for the subsequent Grand Prix of Hungary.
Note in the design of the complete T-tray how Williams opted for a single unit, which also included the initial splitter and the barge boards in front of the sidepods (indicated with arrows) which are usually separated on the other cars.

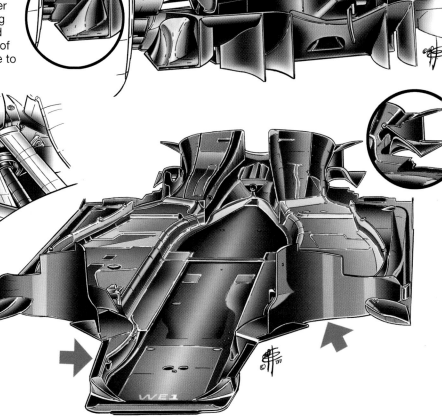

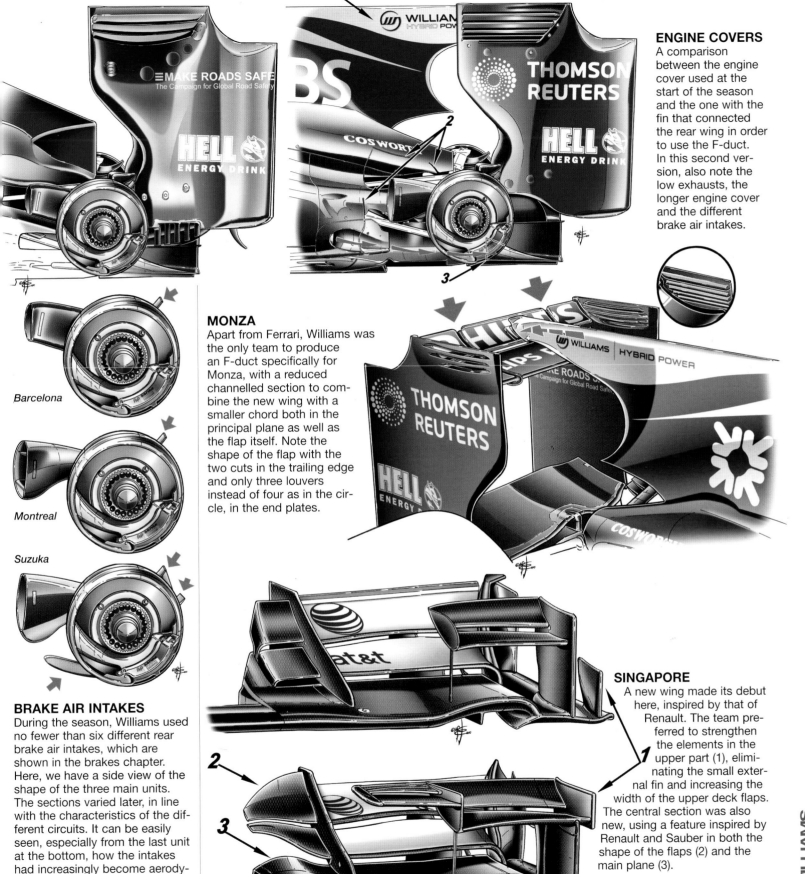

ENGINE COVERS

A comparison between the engine cover used at the start of the season and the one with the fin that connected the rear wing in order to use the F-duct. In this second version, also note the low exhausts, the longer engine cover and the different brake air intakes.

MONZA

Apart from Ferrari, Williams was the only team to produce an F-duct specifically for Monza, with a reduced channelled section to combine the new wing with a smaller chord both in the principal plane as well as the flap itself. Note the shape of the flap with the two cuts in the trailing edge and only three louvers instead of four as in the circle, in the end plates.

Barcelona

Montreal

Suzuka

BRAKE AIR INTAKES

During the season, Williams used no fewer than six different rear brake air intakes, which are shown in the brakes chapter. Here, we have a side view of the shape of the three main units. The sections varied later, in line with the characteristics of the different circuits. It can be easily seen, especially from the last unit at the bottom, how the intakes had increasingly become aerodynamic devices with the added deflectors and fins (arrows) to create downforce.

SINGAPORE

A new wing made its debut here, inspired by that of Renault. The team preferred to strengthen the elements in the upper part (1), eliminating the small external fin and increasing the width of the upper deck flaps. The central section was also new, using a feature inspired by Renault and Sauber in both the shape of the flaps (2) and the main plane (3).

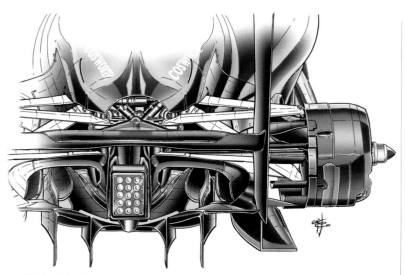

GEARBOX

The Williams FW32 used a gearbox of much contained longitudinal dimensions, which permitted the team to notably reduce the increase in wheelbase caused by the bigger fuel tank, which was enlarged to hold all the petrol necessary for the race. Note the inclination of the wishbones, which allowed the technicians to acquire the suspension's anti-squat values.

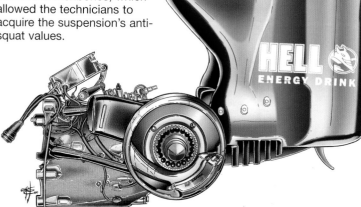

SINGAPORE

The aerodynamic package introduced in Singapore also included a diffuser that was somewhat modified in its central channel, which was made larger and had a different section. The part at the sides of the wheels was also new. Note the two horizontal fins, the task of which was to increase the section of the hole that feeds the double diffuser.

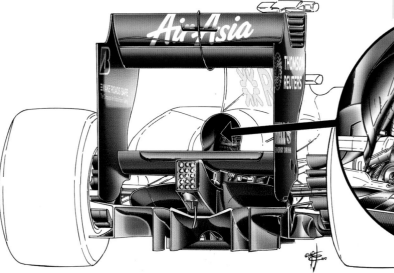

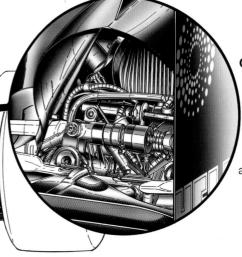

CENTRAL AIR VENT

With the long engine cover version introduced at Silverstone, one of the methods of dissipating heat on hot tracks was to use this large hole. Among other things, the hole facilitated the observation of the complex layout of the rear suspension, which also had transverse inertial dampers.

SUZUKA

The team's last development package of the season concerned the new front and rear brake air intakes, the fronts with the task of improving the circulation of air in the zone around the wheels. A new feature was the downwards extension inspired by a technique brought in by Force India at Monaco and copied at Spa by Renault.
At the rear end, the brake air intakes were subjected to a notable evolution, with the addition of another fin and vertical end plates for the purpose of creating more downforce.
Below, to point out the generally horizontal part around the wheels that has a significantly upwards curved leading edge to benefit from the exhaust blow, which has already been illustrated in the diffuser design introduced at Hockenheim.

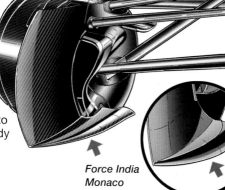

Force India
Monaco

Despite finishing two positions higher in the constructors' championship, the 2010 season still backfired somewhat on Force India, which missed out on two prestigious results.

One was at Spa and the other at Monza: pole position and second behind Raikkonen by Giancarlo Fisichella at the Belgian circuit and first row of the grid in Italy for Adrian Sutil.

The VJM03 turned out to be more effective than its predecessor and was not just at ease on fast circuits in low drags configuration as per Spa and Monza. Like the 2009 VJM02, the 2010 car had a decidedly long wheelbase – second only to that of McLaren – and was powered by the same engine and also same narrow, long gearbox.

That was a factor that determined the length of the 3409 mm wheelbase, with the opportunity of exploiting a vast area in which to create its negative lift effect with double diffusers, of which no fewer than seven were made in different configurations during the season. It was actually the development of the season that slowed Force India, especially in the second half, compared to rivals Renault, Williams and Sauber, even if the Swiss team came immediately after Force India in the final championship table. James Key leaving the team influenced this situation as he moved to Sauber at the start of the season; then Mark Smith migrated to Lotus and that was worsened by the lack of a suitable budget.

The family resemblance to the 2009 car was strong except for the nose, which was less profiled and had a kind of hump in the lower area and a wider, square shape at the point. It was a nose that had undergone development for the fast circuits, resulting in a version like that of the VJM02. The disposition of the front brake calipers was odd, vertical but overhung in respect of the disc. A feature dictated by the characteristics of the front suspension, but not optimum for cooling them. It was in that sector that Force India set a trend with the faring inside the front intakes, introduced at Monaco, which was then copied by other teams as the season went on.

CONSTRUCTORS' CLASSIFICATION		
	2009	2010
Position	9°	7°

Force India VJM02

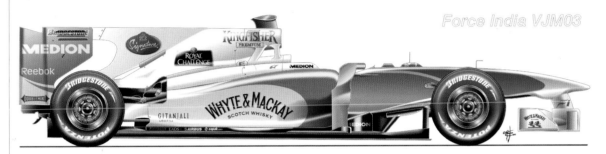

Force India VJM03

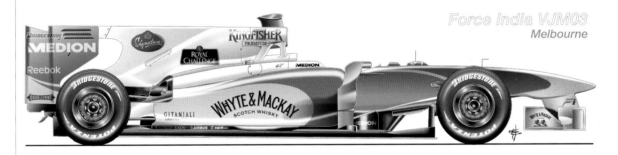

Force India VJM03
Melbourne

Force India VJM03
Montreal

Force India VJM03
Valencia

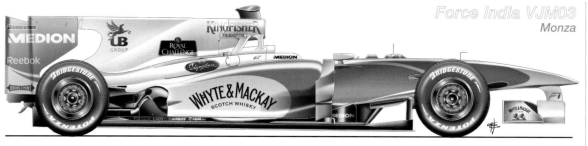

Force India VJM03
Monza

Force India VJM03
Singapore

To Force India goes the credit for having taken a step forward in the interpretation of the McLaren F-duct, fielding a version that blew onto the main plane and not on the flap during practice for the Grand Prix of Turkey, a method attempted by Sauber but with uncertain results. This design ensured greater potential of use, but it was difficult to set up; so much so that it didn't make its consistent race debut until the British GP at Silverstone.

As is always the case it was copied, this time by Renault for Spa, Red Bull for Singapore and McLaren for Suzuka; it should also have been adopted by Ferrari, but in the end Maranello preferred to put its money on the much tried and tested blow in the flap for the last few races. Other features introduced by Force India included the positioning of the television camera in the low central area inside the pillars of the front wing at Istanbul, which was even copied by Red Bull at Silverstone. The race debut of the low exhausts, the other element that set a trend in 2010, did not happen until Spa after having first appeared at Hockenheim during Friday's sessions.

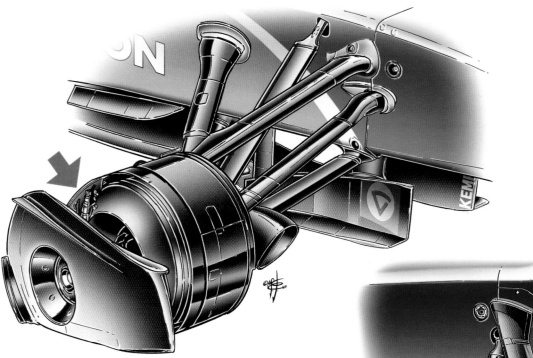

BRAKES

The unique position of the front end's brake calipers switched from the classic position at the top of the VJM02's disc to the lower end of the unit.

They were slightly inclined to privilege the kinematic mechanism of the suspension, to the detriment of their cooling efficiency. Note the large external rim covers, which were outlawed for 2010.

MELBOURNE

The regulation of the front flap's incidence did not happen until the second race of the season, as can be seen in the illustration. New noses with wider vertical supports (visible in the profile) arrived on the Friday afternoon in Australia and were similar to the ones Mercedes-Benz took to Bahrain.

MONACO

This notable evolution of the brake air intakes was introduced at Monte Carlo. It was extensive and curved near the front to better channel the air flow towards the lower area of the car. A solution that set a trend as the season progressed.

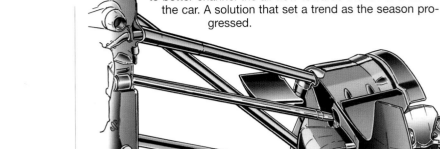

ISTANBUL

Another feature that set a trend was the low, central position of the television camera, which formed a sort of added mini-plane to better channell the air to the car's lower area. Introduced in Istanbul, it was also used at Silverstone in parallel with a similar solution copied by Red Bull.

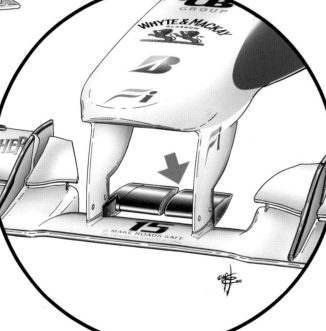

F-DUCT

The F-duct also made its debut in Istanbul, but in practice. This one was completely new, with the blow on the main plane instead of the flap, ensuring greater efficiency and exploitation but also more set-up difficulty, a factor that delayed its use on both cars in the British GP race at Silverstone. This F-duct, introduced at the Grand Prix of Australia by Sauber, was then copied by Renault, Red Bull and McLaren.

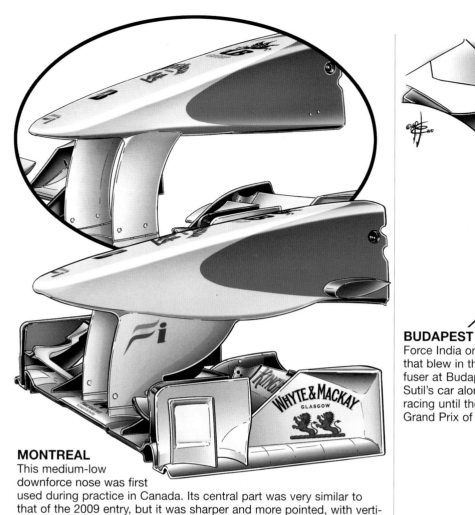

BUDAPEST

Force India only fitted low exhausts that blew in the lateral channels of the diffuser at Budapest and did so as an experiment on Sutil's car alone on the Friday. Neither car had them for racing until the subsequent Grand Prix of Belgium.

MONTREAL

This medium-low downforce nose was first used during practice in Canada. Its central part was very similar to that of the 2009 entry, but it was sharper and more pointed, with vertical pillars that were narrower and without the hump in the lower area. Note the similarity of the front wing's end plates, which were split like the 2009 version.

MONZA

Two rear wings were available at Monza. One was the same as at Spa with an F-duct and cut flap chord and the other had no F-duct and was based on planes used in 2009. The latter's principal plane was of reduced chord (1) and flap with a central Gurney flap (2) used in the race; this configuration had no small upside down U-shaped plane (3) above the deformable structure.

The 2010 was a diffi-
cult season for
Sauber, although the start was
positive. Two factors conditioned
the team's year: the abandonment of BMW just when it was
constructing its new car; they
had already built the new gearbox. The other was the loss of
Willy Rampf, the technical leader
of the Swiss team. After the 2010
car had been finished and the
third race of the season was on
the cards, his place was taken by
James Key, ex-technical boss of
Jordan, whose 2009 Force India
car was the revelation of that
season. The BMW engine gave
way to the 8-cylinder Ferrari,
which came with its own transmission and that gave the team
yet another headache, because
they had to abandon a system
that was, by then, well tried and
tested. Compared to the 2009
car, the 2010 Sauber had a
wheelbase about 14 cm longer
and it had lost the angular shape
of its front wing, partly because
the starting point of the new project was the version introduced
in Singapore with a nose that
broke away from that of its predecessor.
Sauber has to be credited with
being the first team to have
adopted the experimental F-duct,
which had been tested since the
season's second race.
This thanks to the fact that the
team had already followed
McLaren with the blown rear
wing – even if the task of this
development was the opposite of
the F-duct – from the 2009
Grand Prix of Singapore.
The system brought in on the
C29 in Australia revealed itself to
be rather complicated, with the
duct for its operation fitted to the
left sidepod. A new and more
efficient version was produced
for the Spanish GP, with the duct
in the front part of the chassis,
like the McLaren. James Key was
immediately productive as soon
as he arrived, in part because
Force India in its low resistance
configuration was considered
one of the best cars from the
aerodynamics point of view,
which became the Achilles heel
of the Sauber, a car that also did
not have great traction and
lacked stability due to set-ups
that were too rigid.
The notable opportunities offered
by the Swiss team's wind tunnel

CONSTRUCTORS' CLASSIFICATION		
	2009	2010
Position	6°	8°

BMW-Sauber F109

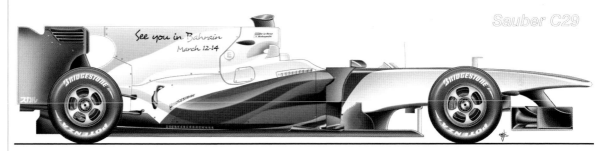

Sauber C29

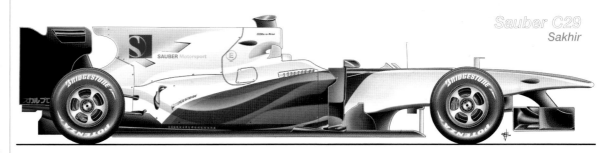

Sauber C29
Sakhir

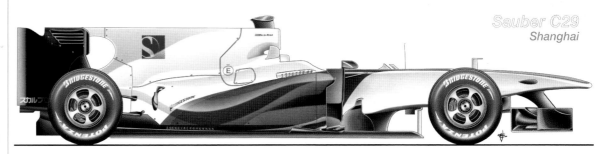

Sauber C29
Shanghai

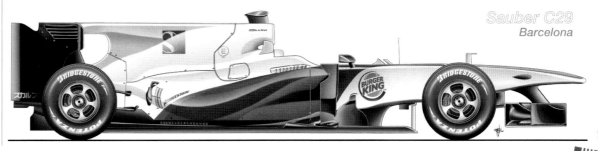

Sauber C29
Barcelona

did the rest, contributing to a substantial recovery of performance during the rest of the season. There was a certain lack of Ferrari engine reliability but, strangely, only with Pedro De La Rosa's car and that slowed development during the first part of the season.

But development there was and it took place in five fundamental stages: the new F-duct and suspension made their debut at Barcelona; diffuser and brake air intakes at Valencia; the front wing at Silverstone; a Red Bull-type front wing and diffuser at Hockenheim; and the definitive diffuser at Singapore.

As the team had a limited budget, Key decided against exhausts blowing into the diffusers, partially because his complex design and creation meant the system would not have appeared until the Grand Prix of Japan, the third last race of the season, diverting too much energy from the design of the 2011 car. One of the strong points of the Swiss team was the car's braking system, which also had a smaller but most efficient air intake in terms of resistance to the forward feed of the front end. The rear of the car followed the fashionable multiplication of winglets – like those of Williams, illustrated in the Brakes chapter – to create downforce.

Sauber C29
Montreal

Sauber C29
Hockenheim

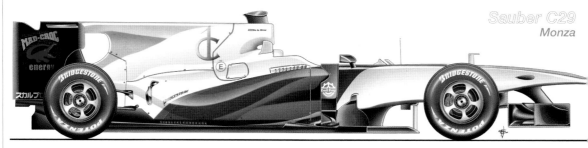

Sauber C29
Monza

Sauber C29
Singapore

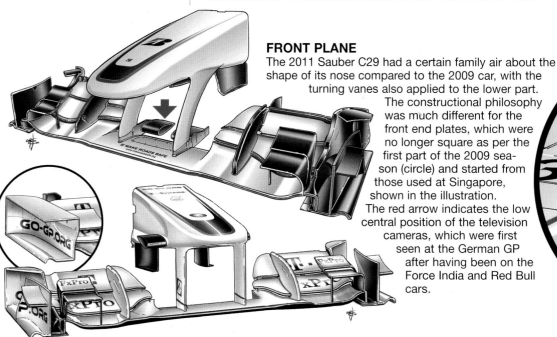

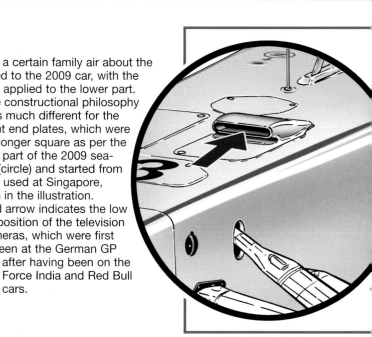

FRONT PLANE

The 2011 Sauber C29 had a certain family air about the shape of its nose compared to the 2009 car, with the turning vanes also applied to the lower part.

The constructional philosophy was much different for the front end plates, which were no longer square as per the first part of the 2009 season (circle) and started from those used at Singapore, shown in the illustration.

The red arrow indicates the low central position of the television cameras, which were first seen at the German GP after having been on the Force India and Red Bull cars.

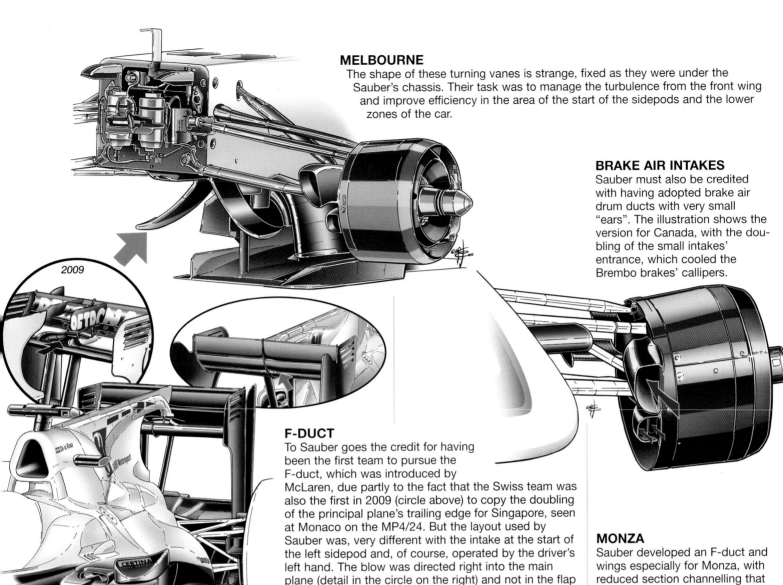

MELBOURNE
The shape of these turning vanes is strange, fixed as they were under the Sauber's chassis. Their task was to manage the turbulence from the front wing and improve efficiency in the area of the start of the sidepods and the lower zones of the car.

2009

BRAKE AIR INTAKES
Sauber must also be credited with having adopted brake air drum ducts with very small "ears". The illustration shows the version for Canada, with the doubling of the small intakes' entrance, which cooled the Brembo brakes' callipers.

F-DUCT
To Sauber goes the credit for having been the first team to pursue the F-duct, which was introduced by McLaren, due partly to the fact that the Swiss team was also the first in 2009 (circle above) to copy the doubling of the principal plane's trailing edge for Singapore, seen at Monaco on the MP4/24. But the layout used by Sauber was, very different with the intake at the start of the left sidepod and, of course, operated by the driver's left hand. The blow was directed right into the main plane (detail in the circle on the right) and not in the flap like the MP4/25. But it was dropped because it needed more setting up compared to the flap blow.

MONZA
Sauber developed an F-duct and wings especially for Monza, with reduced section channelling that influenced the flap, which also had a smaller chord. Note the end plates with just one gill. As can be seen from the illustration, the exhausts were in the high position throughout the season.

F-DUCT CONTROL
At the Grand Prix of Spain the means of feeding the F-duct with an intake on the sidepod was dropped in favour of the same method as McLaren: one of the two windows for access to the pedals. The blow reached the flap rather than the principal plane. The driver operated it with his left hand in a slightly different way, no longer laterally but forwards to close the hole.

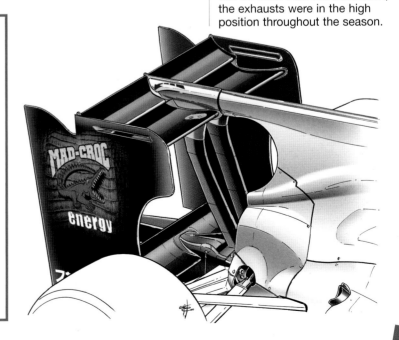

All in all, the 2010 season was positive for Toro Rosso despite the logistical difficulty of having to operate from a headquarters in Faenza, Italy but with a wind tunnel, which was not up to the latest standards, at Bicester, England. To this must be added both a technical office and aerodynamic department a long way from the level of their adversaries. Not only did development suffer but also the conception of the car itself, which was a simple but correct evolution of the 2009 version without the introduction of the major new developments that appeared on many of the 2010 cars.

The longer wheelbase to host a tank that could carry the fuel necessary to cover the whole race distance was, in part, compensated for by a decidedly short gearbox. So the monocoque was long and narrow, but it was the short transmission box that partially compromised the chance of an ample volume for the double diffuser, where the car's Red Bull RB6 cousin adopted a narrow, long and even raised gearbox in relation to the reference plane. Due to logistical and budget necessities, Toro Rosso had to bring forward the construction of the first monocoque to September, so restricting all the rest of the project with a basic penalisation. At the launch, the STR5 had the same low exhausts as the 2009 Red Bull, but from the first race of the season the team went back to the traditional type as they waited to bring in the diffuser blown project during the season. Toro Rosso also retained the pull rod rear suspension layout, as they did the prone brake calipers (Brembo) at the front like the Red Bull RB6.

Of the two new developments that set the trend in the 2010 season, Giorgio Ascanelli preferred to push the exhausts rather than the F-duct – which was going to be banned at the end of the year – partly because they would serve as a study basis for the 2011 car.

Toro Rosso STR4

Toro Rosso STR5

Toro Rosso STR5

Sakhir

Toro Rosso STR5

Montreal

Toro Rosso STR5

Budapest

CONSTRUCTORS' CLASSIFICATION		
	2009	2010
Position	10°	9°

Toro Rosso STR5
Monza

Toro Rosso STR5
Singapore

The blown diffusers with low exhausts first appeared at Monza, a GP late in relation to expectations, because the ideal track would have been Spa.

The F-duct layout was also brought in during Monza practice, but it never went beyond the debut stage due to set-up difficulties related to the first phase of its use. Faenza immediately opted for the more sophisticated and powerful version first fielded by Force India at Silverstone, with the blow directly onto the main plane instead of the flap, which was copied by Renault (Spa), Red Bull (Singapore) and McLaren (Suzuka).

We have added this version in the review of planes even though it never raced.

CHASSIS AND BRAKE AIR INTAKES

The shape of the STR5's chassis was similar to that of the 2009 car (circle). In fact, it was identical in the lower zone, but had two more pronounced "horns" in the upper area.

The brake air intakes were highly sophisticated: as well as the two bigger mouths to cool the discs and the one for the prone callipers (below), there was a fin to direct the air flow towards the lower part of the car.

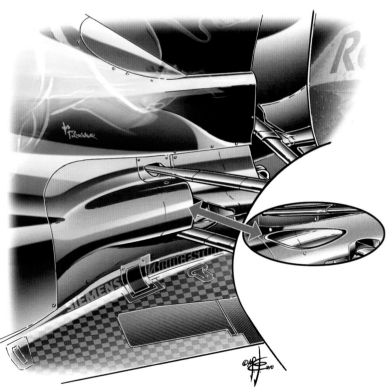

SEPANG

A body with a fairing first tested at Bahrain with its relative air vent in the exhaust area was used in its original form in Melbourne (circle) to improve the evacuation of heat, but it was never seen again after the Australian GP.

MONACO

Toro Rosso and Sauber were the only teams to fit a middle-wing above the lower plane and was 15 cm wide, as permitted by the regulations. Note the blown flap above in the central zone.

BUDAPEST

A new nose appeared on the Toro Rosso in Hungary with two large vertical panels (1) applied to the sides, which hid the original shape, and was much tapered to produce more vertical load. The new end plates introduced at Silverstone were modified with an added blower (2), as well as the Renault-style longitudinal unit (3). A Gurney flap was added to the second unit to increase downforce. In the circle is the end plate that first appeared in Turkey with its lower area completely flat (5), a small internal finlet (6) and a different cascade wing (7).

DIFFUSER

Seen from below, the Toro Rosso's diffuser can be easily seen and was not one of the most extreme: (1) in the lateral channels there are four large middle vanes (two per part) and two small units (2). (3) The sealing zone inside the wheels is curved and raised.

Red Bull 2009

F-DUCT

Introduced at the Italian circuit as an experiment, the Toro Rosso F-duct was systematically tested in all subsequent race weekends, but without it being promoted to race use. Different from those of all the other cars, the air entered through a central mouth that interrupts the line of the engine cover. The blow took place directly onto the central plane and that should have ensured greater efficiency, but instead it complicated the car's delicate set-up.

MONZA

Toro Rosso took two important new developments to Italy: the F-duct, which was only used in practice, and low exhausts that blew into the lateral channels à la Red Bull and which were actually used in the race. The illustration shows the new units, which were adopted without modifying the body that still had the old fairing for high exhausts (above).

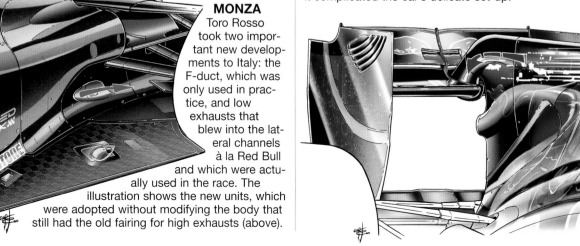

With the retirement of BMW and Toyota at the end of 2009, the number of teams that would have taken to the grid dropped to nine, so there would only have been 18 cars at the start of each Grand Prix. To avoid such a situation, the Federation allowed three new teams to compete for the Formula 1 World Championship, guaranteeing them a Cosworth engine and an X-Trac gearbox, even if Virgin eventually designed and produced its own transmission. Problems of budget, especially for HRT, timing and structure meant that the three teams came up with cars that were not of a current F1 technical level. That is why, during a season with such a wealth of technical innovation coming from the established teams, it was decided to devote the usual number of pages to the various chapters of this book, reducing somewhat the

amount of space given to the newcomers which, particularly in HRT's case, carried out little or no aerodynamic updates during the season. Suffice it to say that the Spanish team went to all the rounds in the world championship with the same front and rear wings, brake air intakes and its technical personnel structure that was much reduced. Clearly, all three teams regarded 2010 as a series of tests for the 2011 season, for which we expected a step forward in quality, especially from Lotus, which brought back such a prestigious F1 name, a symbol of progress and avant garde development.

Of the three teams, Lotus started out with the most solid basis. It had a technician with extensive experience in F1 like Mike Gascoyne, a cohesive working group – even if it was made up of just six people – track technicians and engineers from Toyota and with the support of Jean Claude Migeot, plus the Aerolab wind tunnel.
The disadvantages were the fact that they signed a collaboration contract on 12 June and took possession of their headquarters on 4 September; in addition, the working group was expanded to 25 people, most of them ex-Toyota technicians. In fact, Lotus started up when the other Formula 1 teams were already moving ahead creating the first components for the 2010 season. Result: a very, very conventional car at least two seasons behind the opposition and which, obviously, had to be used as a mobile test laboratory for their 2011 programme. The fairly contained wheelbase and a fuel tank that exploited the maximum permitted width contributed to creating the impression of a very solid, square car. There were many reliability problems with the gearbox's hydraulic components but, despite everything, Lotus was, perhaps, the minor team that had developed the most.
The first package of updates arrived at Barcelona, together with a programme for lightening the car that slimmed it down by about 20 kg. The second set of developments appeared at Silverstone, with aerodynamic elements including a front wing that recalled those of the 2009 Toyota. Nevertheless, the car was always over one and a half seconds behind the other teams and without any hope of being able to make ninth place in the constructors' championship.
But to Gascoyne's team went the "honour" of being the first of the last three in the table!

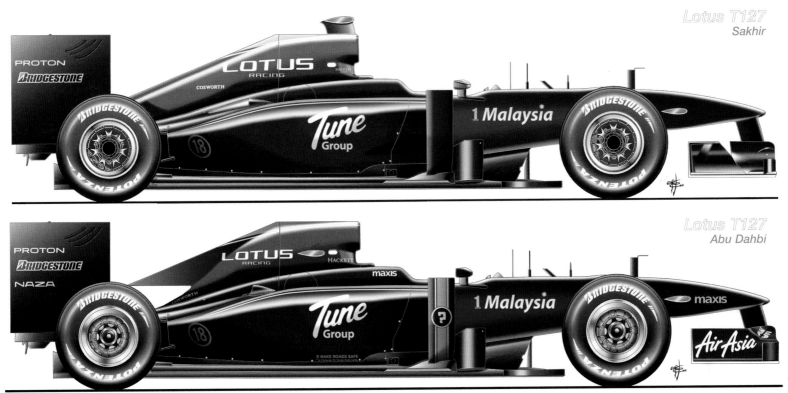

Lotus T127
Sakhir

Lotus T127
Abu Dahbi

HRT

In presenting this team, it is sufficient to say just one thing: the final assembly of their cars took place in their Bahrain garage at the season's first race weekend. So without covering a single metre of private testing in preparation for the season! Budget problems meant the creation of the car at Dallara was littered with stops and starts, which distorted the initial project. Just think that HRT ran the early races with steel suspension, their cars being fitted with the carbon fibre version much later for the Grand Prix of Spain.

Geoff Willis belatedly arrived to direct the operation from the pits, but despite his great experience he was held up by insurmountable budget problems that allowed no aerodynamic development during the entire season.

The enormous reliability problems linked to the new X-Trac gearbox hydraulics convinced the team to reach a transmission supply agreement with Williams for 2011. HRT tried to work towards better reliability with new hydraulic components, which first appeared at the Spanish GP.

A new system of fuel acquisition and a tank supplied by ATL made their debut at the Grand Prix of Great Britain. Lack of aerodynamic development increasingly penalised the developing car as the season wore on, especially because the other teams continued to improve, while HRT found it impossible to solve chronic understeer problems without adequate aerodynamic progress, which could not be made due to a lack of budget.

HRT
Sakhir

HRT
Abu Dahbi

Virgin takes the last place in this review, not only because of its results but for the ambitious statements made by Nick Wirth, the technical head of the team, which obviously failed.

The ambition of being able to create a tunnel car based solely on a study carried out with CFD and without a wind tunnel clashed with the level of competitiveness of the other F1 teams.

As well as that, Virgin was not very reliable, experiencing no fewer than four suspensions breakdowns, which made them meditate on driver safety. In addition, Virgin was the only team to get its fuel tank capacity wrong. A factor that forced it to build two new monocoques, lengthened by "only" 135 mm…

This obviously increased the wheelbase, with an immediate worsening of performance, from which it slowly recovered with a new aerodynamic package for Silverstone, immediately followed by a second for the subsequent race at Hockenheim.

Other small developments continued until the Korean GP.

Virgin VR01
Sakhir

Virgin VR01
Abu Dahbi

The season opened with many new developments. We have never previously seen so many different cars with such new and revolutionary technical features. The interesting thing is that the new ideas were not just the preserve of two or a maximum of three teams, as is usually the case, but many more. McLaren, Renault, Williams, Toro Rosso have all opened up new roads even if in some cases this meant a return to old solutions with a leap back 20 years into the past, as did Red Bull in 2009. Such is the case with the L-shaped McLaren sidepods, similar to those of the 1996 F310, and the double underbody of the Ferrari F92 that was "revisited" by Toro Rosso.

The pull rod rear suspension was spread liberally among another six of the 2011 contenders as well as Red Bull and Toro Rosso, who gave the feature its debut in 2009. Even stragglers Lotus, HRT and Virgin created projects that should no longer be inferior to GP2 cars, which was the case in 2010. Top of the list of new developments are Renault's advanced exhausts, not just because they were a real surprise, but especially because they brought with them a whole series of complications that required careful, extensive study. The team's engine specialists had to resolve difficult problems so as not to lose out in terms of engine efficiency, with an exhaust terminal angled forward and over a metre long. Second place goes to McLaren with its L-shaped sidepods, which meant a notable revolution of the architecture of components hidden under the bodywork, while the other new development of exhausts with multiple terminals never got past track testing. The miniaturised rear end of the Williams was a brave move, with the differential box so low that they were forced to introduce a drive shafts angle of about 14°, which was previously considered impossible; upper wishbone anchorage to a the vertical wing support was also new. Result: while the car was being built with an extremely low rear end, the FW31's even dropped below that of the Red Bull RB7 by about 2 cm.

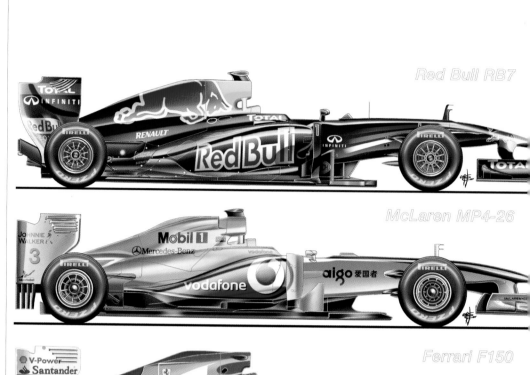

Red Bull RB7

McLaren MP4-26

Ferrari F150

Mercedes MGP W02

Renault RE31

Williams FW33

Force India VJM04

Sauber C30

Toro Rosso STR06

HRT F111

Lotus T128

Virgin MVR02

The latter, the top 2011 car, did not cause a stir at its presentation, because Adrian Newey's great revolution had already taken place in 2009. In fact, the new RB7 drew more from the 2009 car than it did from the 2010 world championship winner.

The Ferrari F150 Italia did not amaze people either at its launch or in its final form with the latest developments at its first race.

It immediately seemed like an intelligent evolution of the old F10 but too traditional, especially in a season like the 2011 in which everyone fielded extreme cars.

The F150 Italia was the only top team car to stay loyal to the push rod suspension layout – as did Sauber, but they were obliged to do so, because they use the same Ferrari engine and gearbox – HRT and Virgin.

The pursuit of the RB7 started at the very first race, with McLaren the star of an exceptional recovery from the opening race in Australia and the British squad was the only one to fight Red Bull for victory in Melbourne.

This first 2011 review was stopped at the Grand Prix of Germany by the great technical revolution brought in by the Federation, starting at Valencia, concerning engine mapping and the choking of the exhausts' hot blow, culminating in the clear-cut victory of Alonso and his Ferrari at Silverstone.

This latest regulation was then abolished at the subsequent German GP, in which McLaren made its comeback but Ferrari was able to hold off Red Bull. The new technical development arrived with an experiment conducted by Renault and the indirect rejection of one of the surprises of the season: exhausts that blew into the front parts of the sidepods. On Heidfeld's car, they exited at the rear as on the Red Bull, but highlighted problems created by the original project.

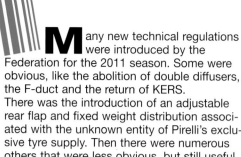

Many new technical regulations were introduced by the Federation for the 2011 season. Some were obvious, like the abolition of double diffusers, the F-duct and the return of KERS.

There was the introduction of an adjustable rear flap and fixed weight distribution associated with the unknown entity of Pirelli's exclusive tyre supply. Then there were numerous others that were less obvious, but still useful for limiting the extent of aerodynamics and reducing the so-called grey areas in the text, which had often sparked off arguments the previous season. These are shown in this illustration of the 2010 world championship winning car to facilitate the identification.

We will limit ourselves to illustrating some of them in detail, using the technical regulation articles texts themselves.

In the diagrams there are examples of how much was done during the 2010 season in getting around the content of the regulations in some cases.

DOUBLE DIFFUSERS PROHIBITED *DIS 1-1B*

ART. 3.12.9
In the zone within 450 mm of the centreline and the one delimited in a longitudinal sense between 450 mm in front of the rear end plate of the cockpit opening and 350 mm behind the rear axle, every intersection visible from below with vertical lateral or longitudinal planes must form a continuous line. The only aperture permitted is that in article 3.12.7 of the regulations (for access to the starter).

In the illustration it can be easily seen how pedantic was the question of double diffusers. Just a slot of a few millimetres in the body would be enough to legalise a hole of larger dimensions, which fed the double diffusers for the regulation stating that, observing the car from below, one must be able to see the sky.

ART. 3.12.10
In the zone within 650 mm of the centreline and in the delimited area in a longitudinal sense between 450 mm ahead of the rear end plates of the cockpit aperture and 350 mm behind the rear axle, every intersection of the body visible from below with vertical lateral or longitudinal planes must form a continuous line.

ART. 3.12.11
The verification of these norms must be made without taking into account (Art. 15.4.8.) the unsuspended mass (elements of the suspension).

MINIMUM WEIGHT
The minimum weight of a 2011 car was raised from 620 kg to 640 kg following the return of KERS and the increased chassis safety measures.

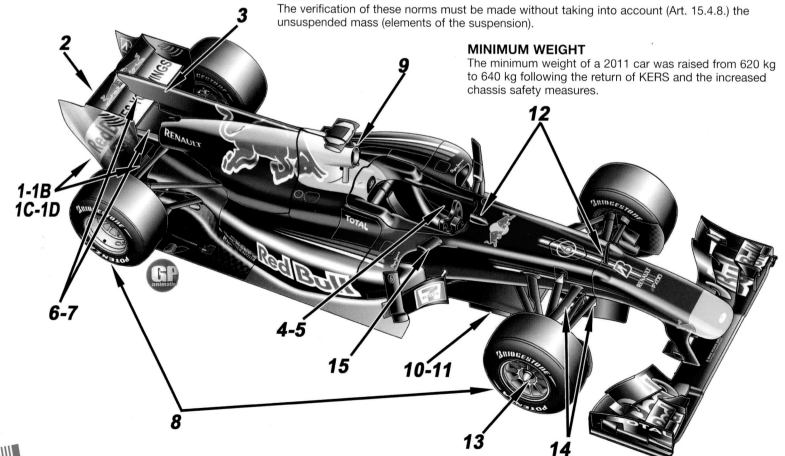

STARTER HOLE REGULATION *DIS 1 C*
ART. 3.12.7
There may be an aperture in the central channel of the diffuser giving access to the starter motor, the area of which may not be more than 3500 mm², and every point of the aperture may not be further than 100 mm from any other point of that aperture.

ADJUSTABLE REAR WING FLAP (DRS) *DIS 2*
ART. 3.18.1
The upper closed section (flap) of the rear wing may be modified in its incidence when the car is moving. No other component (apart from those necessary for the car's movement) in contact with the air flow may be positioned more than 355 mm from the centreline.
Every incidence variation must respect the regulation in force concerning the body. The system must make the flap return to its original position in the case of an anomaly. The variation of incidence must be controlled by the driver upon authorisation from the race director (Art.3.18.2). The on/off control may only be used when the car is less than a second from the one that precedes it.
The variations of incidence must be neutralised each time the driver operates the brakes.

50mm
10mm

LIMITATIONS OF THE REAR WING SUPPORTS *DIS 3B*
ART. 3.10.9
The supports of the rear wing may have two closed symmetrical sections with a maximum total area of 5000 mm². The thickness of each of the two sections may not exceed 25 mm. The radius of linkage between these sections and the wing plane (surface defined by Art. 3.10.2) may not exceed 10 mm.

FINS CONNECTED TO THE REAR WING BANNED *DIS 3*
ART. 3.9.1
No part of the car body between 50 mm and 330 mm in front of the rear axle may be higher than 730 mm from the reference plane.

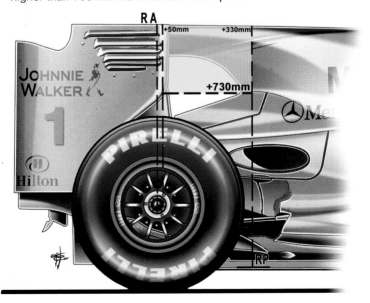
RA
+50mm +330mm
+730mm

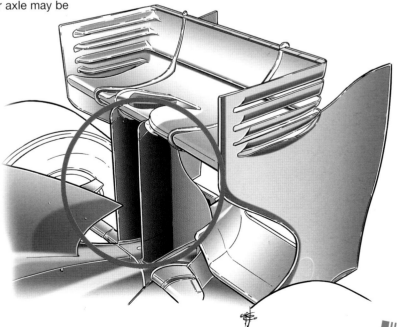

BLOWN REAR WING PROHIBITED *DIS 6*
ART. 3.10.2
The body, in the zone between the 50 mm in front of the rear axle, situated 730 mm above the RP and within 355 mm of the centreline, must be situated in an area which, when seen from the side, is between the rear axle and 350 mm behind it.

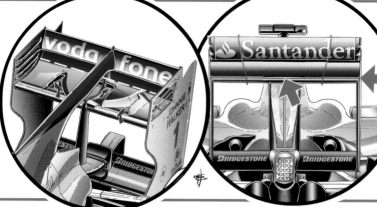

ART. 3.18
From the side view, there may not be more than two sections, each completely closed. No part of these two sections in contact with the air flow may have a concave radius of curvature inferior to 100 mm. A Gurney flap may be added to the trailing edge of a maximum of 20 mm. The chord of the higher section must always be less than the chord of the lower one.

F-DUCT CONTROL BY DRIVER PROHIBITED
DIS 4-5
ART. 3.15
Apart from the devices used for the regulation of the car as described in Art. 3.18, any body movement by the driver suspected of influencing the car's aerodynamics is prohibited.

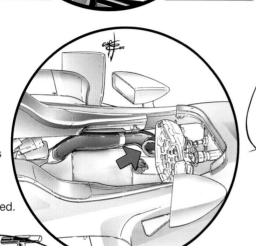

BLOWN BEAM WING PROHIBITED *DIS 7*
ART. 3.10.1
In the zone situated more than 150 mm from the rear axle, at a height of between 150 mm and 730 mm from the PR and between 75 mm and 355 mm from the centreline line, the body must be in a limited area of between 150 mm and 350 mm from the rear axle, and between 300 mm and 400 mm above the RP. In a lateral view, the section may have one single element. Only adding of a Gurney flap is permitted and that must not exceed 20 mm.

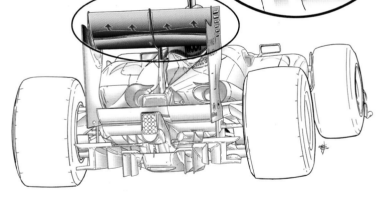

MANDATORY WEIGHT DISTRIBUTION *DIS 8*
ART. 4.2
Only for the 2011 season, the weight measured on the front and rear wheels must not exceed 201 kg and 342 kg respectively during qualifying (weighing to be carried out with slick tyres). Weight distribution must vary between 53.3% and 54.5% at the front end and 45.5% and 46.7% at the rear.

KNIFE EDGE ROLL BAR LIMITATIONS *DIS 9*
ART. 15.4
The roll bar for the protection of the driver must have a minimum closed area of 10.000 mm^2 in its vertical projection, measured in a flat place at 50 mm above its highest point. Its dimensions in length and width may not exceed 200 mm, with a minimum thickness of 10.000 mm^2.

53.3/54.5
min 342kg (Q)

45.5/46.7
min291kg (Q)

FLEXIBLE SPLITTER PROHIBITED
DIS 10-10B
ART. 3.17.5
The body may have a maximum vertical flexing of 5 mm under a push of 2000 N applied at three different points (one in the centre and two at 100 mm from the centre). The bib splitter under the chassis must be rigidly fixed and must not contain any mechanism that permits non-linear flexing during the verification test.

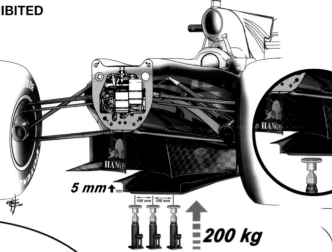

5 mm↑

200 kg

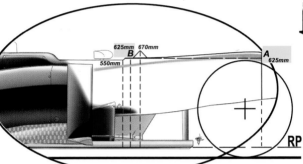

CHASSIS HEIGHT
DIS 11
ART. 15.4.4
The maximum height of the chassis in the sections A-A and B-B may not exceed 625 mm from the RP.

DOUBLING THE WHEEL RETENTION CABLES *DIS 14*
ART. 10.3.6
To avoid the wheels becoming detached, the fixing cables must have a section greater than 110 mm². Each wheel must have two fixing cables, which pass inside each of the suspension arms, with separate attachments to both the chassis and the upright. Each cable must be longer than 450 mm and be able to resist a force of 70 kN applied in each direction.

REAR DEFORMABLE STRUCTURE LIMITATIONS *DIS 13*
ART. 15.2.4
From a lateral view, the rear deformable structure in the area above 50 mm from the rear axle must be contained in a zone that does not vertically exceed 275 mm.

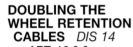

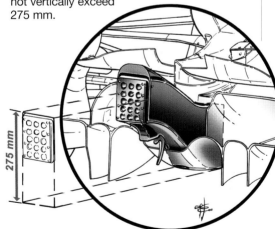

275 mm

AERODYNAMIC RIMS PROHIBITED *DIS 12*
ART. 12.4.6
In the lateral view of the area included between 120 mm and 270 mm in diameter, the rims may not have an area greater than 24.000 mm². That did not stop Ferrari and McLaren producing rims that recalled those of the F10, even if with a smaller ring.

POSITION OF THE MIRRORS
DIS 15
ART. 14.3.3
All the rear view mirror components, including their fixings, must be contained in an area of between 250 mm and 500 mm from the centreline line and at 750 mm from the rear limit of the cockpit opening.

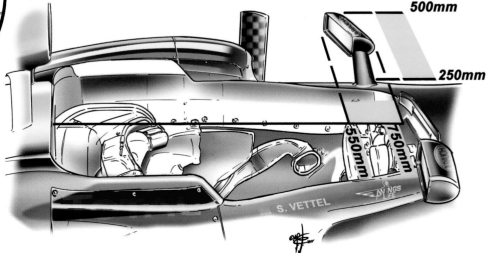

500mm

250mm

FERRARI F150: TOP VIEW COMPARISON

The differences with the old F10, even in its launch version, seen from above. The nose was higher and combined with old front wing introduced at Silverstone. 1) The new developments began with the front suspension and steering arms not incorporated in the upper wishbone fairing for the first time.

2) The driver was slightly more forward; the hoop that shaped the seat back was that from which the position of the slightly raised bust was derived to ensure good visibility. Among other things, that made more space for fuel tank capacity without influencing wheelbase dimensions. 3) The sidepod fronts were different, with inlets much raised and with a rectangular horizontal shape. Lateral deformable structures had been increased. 4) The zone in front of the wheels was considerably narrower compared to the F10; the exhausts blew down low, but they were not the definitive version. 5) The whole damper and torsion bar package had been advanced and miniaturised to create a substantially reduced rear area, as can be seen from the notable inclination of the pull rod link, to obtain some Red Bull-type the advantages. 6) In practice, the rear terminated in an extremely narrow V to ensure greater air flow efficiency to the rear wing and diffusers. 7) The rear wing was only the first experiment with which to test the mechanisms of the adjustable flap.

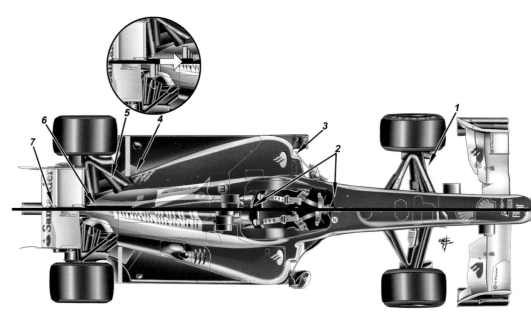

FERRARI STEERING 'WHEEL'

The different driving position meant the development of a steering 'wheel' that was flatter compared to that of the F10 (the difference is shown in yellow) to make more room for the drivers' knees. The most significant new elements were at the rear of the wheel, which boasted new paddles; they took the total to six at the front of the Ferrari F150's steering wheel. The buttons that can be clearly seen at the top were new and needed to operate the adjustable flap (left index finger) and the KERS. Below right is the seventh paddle, the purpose of which was kept secret.

SIDE VIEW: MELBOURNE

1) At the first race of the season, Ferrari fielded the definitive version of the F150 Italia. The most obvious new developments were these two large fins to which the front wing was connected, one that was new in all its components, as were the end plates (2). The initial parts (3) of the sidepods were considerably more concave, with a doubling of the vertical inlets (4) in the low area. In profile, the narrowing of the body was given away by a more expansive surface (5) of insulation material. The body (6) was slightly longer and from it exited the long terminals (7) instead of the basic short version (below). The diffusers (8) were, of course, new, as was the integration between the body and the rear wing support.

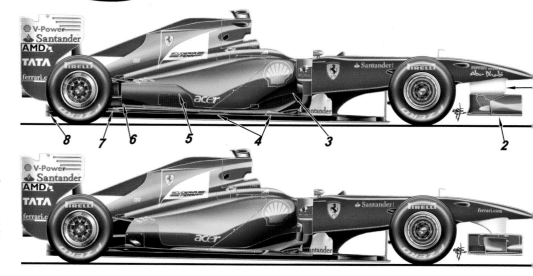

FERRARI EXHAUSTS

In pre-season testing, Ferrari modified the rear of the F150's body. It became slightly longer, the exhausts were moved back and "squashed" to blow towards the centre, where a horizontal cut had been made in the area of the diffuser that generated much curiosity. But the exhausts became the same as those of the Red Bull for the first race of the season.

2

1

McLAREN

McLaren also went back into the past for their new sidepods, the lower areas of which were closed. The large L-shape brought back memories of Rory Byrne's Benetton B 195 – but these were higher at the sides and low in the central area – as well as the even more extreme 'pods of the 1996 Ferrari F310 designed by John Barnard. The concept had been taken to the extreme with the MP4-26 to be able to create an air channel towards the rear able to work in unison with the lower elements of the rear wing. It was a development that brought with it many complications, like the new, long shape of the radiators that were narrow and also L-shaped.

RENAULT

After 28 years, Renault brought in a new and revolutionary element as far as the exhausts were concerned. In 1983, the RE30 taken to Monaco had exhausts that blew straight into the diffuser. In 2011, the RE31's exhausts blew into the front part of the sidepods to energise the air flow in the lower area of the car.

They were partially hidden by the turning vanes, positioned at the sides of the sidepod entrances. To do so, the exhausts were more or less turned upside down, a technique introduced by Ferrari in 2005 and taken up by many teams in 2009.

F 2005

F10

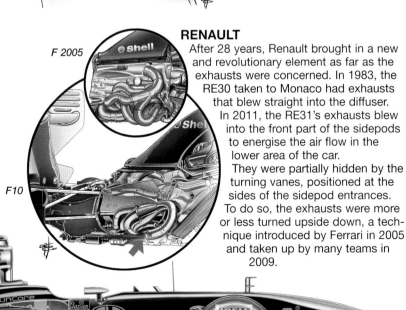

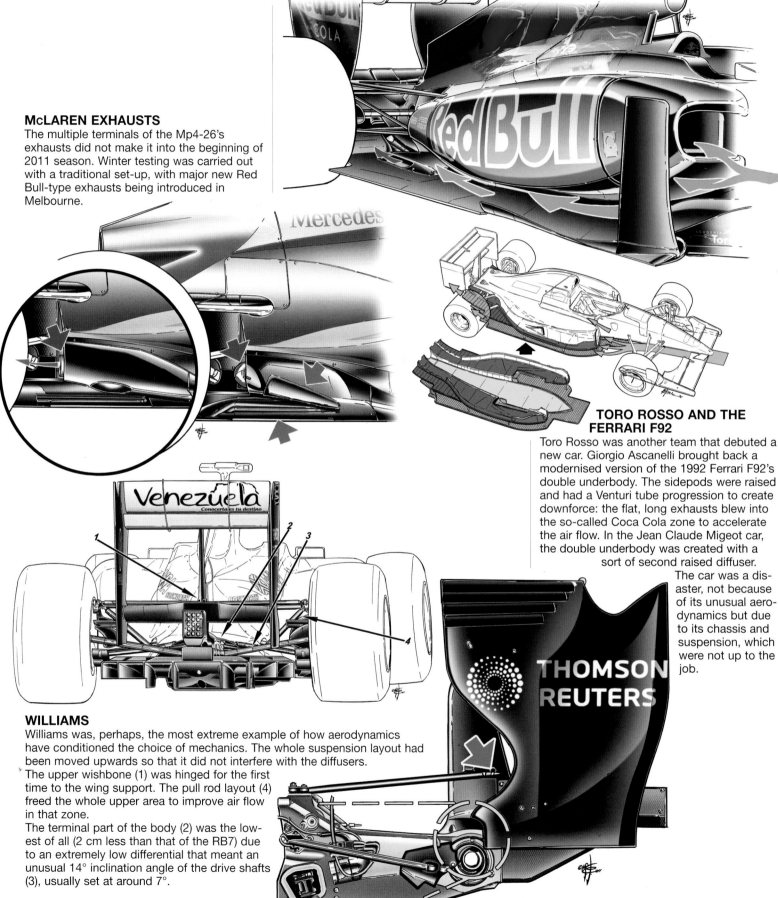

McLAREN EXHAUSTS

The multiple terminals of the Mp4-26's exhausts did not make it into the beginning of 2011 season. Winter testing was carried out with a traditional set-up, with major new Red Bull-type exhausts being introduced in Melbourne.

TORO ROSSO AND THE FERRARI F92

Toro Rosso was another team that debuted a new car. Giorgio Ascanelli brought back a modernised version of the 1992 Ferrari F92's double underbody. The sidepods were raised and had a Venturi tube progression to create downforce: the flat, long exhausts blew into the so-called Coca Cola zone to accelerate the air flow. In the Jean Claude Migeot car, the double underbody was created with a sort of second raised diffuser.

The car was a disaster, not because of its unusual aerodynamics but due to its chassis and suspension, which were not up to the job.

WILLIAMS

Williams was, perhaps, the most extreme example of how aerodynamics have conditioned the choice of mechanics. The whole suspension layout had been moved upwards so that it did not interfere with the diffusers.

The upper wishbone (1) was hinged for the first time to the wing support. The pull rod layout (4) freed the whole upper area to improve air flow in that zone.

The terminal part of the body (2) was the lowest of all (2 cm less than that of the RB7) due to an extremely low differential that meant an unusual 14° inclination angle of the drive shafts (3), usually set at around 7°.

RED BULL RB5

The car Red Bull fielded for the 2011 season was mainly derived from the 2009 RB5, of which it retained the prone brake calipers at the front (1), the much inclined disposition of the radiators and the pull rod suspension layout (4). The position of the exhausts (3) and gearbox (5) were new as they were no longer wide and low, but narrow and raised from the ground. The monolithic upper wishbone was, as always, very wide (6).

RED BULL

At the launch, the Red Bull had a small fin on the engine cover, but it was eliminated from the first test. Two exhaust solutions alternated with each other: one similar to that of the RB6 and one with a very long, flat terminal that blew both above and below the lateral channels. To get around the regulation, a part of the diffuser was cut, shown in yellow in the second illustration.

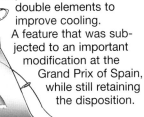

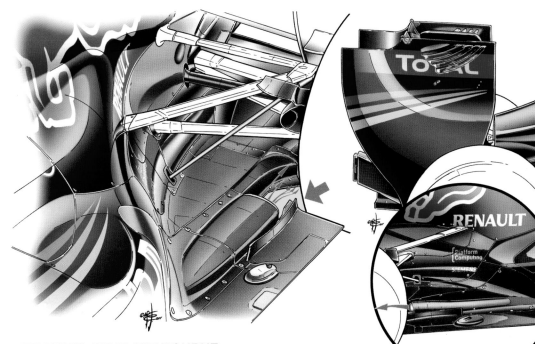

MERCEDES-BENZ: MELBOURNE

The Mercedes-Benz was profoundly modified for the opening race at Melbourne (above). 1) There was a new front wing with a blown plane. 2) The V-shaped turning vane inside the front axle had disappeared, and those at the sides had been modified. 3) Vertical "boomerangs" (4) were introduced in front of the side-pods. And of particular note, the exhaust exit (5) had been moved forward to mid-sidepod and was no longer in front of the rear wheels (below). A number of gills (6-7) had been added to improve cooling. The rear wing and diffuser (8) were new.

MERCEDES-BENZ: RADIATORS

The positioning of the radiators in the Mercedes-Benz' sidepods was new, with their double elements to improve cooling. A feature that was subjected to an important modification at the Grand Prix of Spain, while still retaining the disposition.

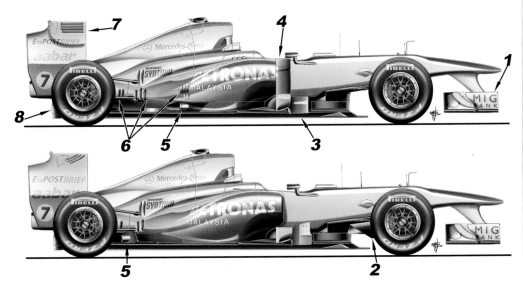

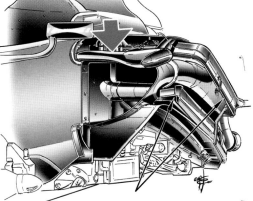

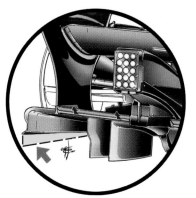

RENAULT STEERING WHEEL

To the seven lever Ferrari steering wheel, Renault responded with one that had eight, featuring two small paddles partly hidden by those of the clutch.
Both were to operate the rear wing flap to ensure easy management with one of the driver's hands, dependent on their position on the wheel – a little like the existing double clutch paddles.
The drivers have always wanted to split them to be sure of being able to work them in the case, for example, of a spin. The two central paddles operate the gearbox, while the two uppers are for the differential as on the 2010 car.

125   **c** = 240 mm   **b** =120mm   +50 mm   **a** = 40mm

RED BULL RAKE

One of the main characteristics of the Red Bull was its highly raked set-up, with the rear end much higher off the ground than the front to create a sort of long Venturi tube. Among other things, the RB7 did not exploit its full ability to descend with the lateral walls as far as the central tunnel level in the area where the exhaust blow is also directed, so that the exhausts acted as thermal mini-skirts. By doing so, they reduced the car's pitch sensitivity, with good downforce especially in relation to the particular set-up of the RB7 on the track. Also note the blow (in yellow in the circle) of the Gurney flap applied to the upper part of the diffuser.

RED BULL: COOLING

With its engine cover off, the Red Bull showed its second body which is almost like a tailor-made suit; its task was to improve the fluid dynamics inside the sidepods. It was all faired so that no mechanical part could cause damaging turbulence. In yellow is the wing plane that acts as a separator between the various thermal dissipation zones. The heat is expelled from two areas: the large hole at the end of the engine cover and the vent low down at the sides of the drive shafts, which interact with the exhaust blow to improve diffuser efficiency.

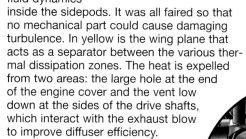

McLAREN

McLaren did an incredible amount of work just before the first race of the season, when the B-version of the MP4-26 appeared. The exhausts were of the Red Bull-type, with a revision of the whole rear of the car. Given the impossibility of being supplied in time by Pyrossic, producers of a special insulation material used in such cases, the team opted for a diffuser in titanium in rapid prototype form.

McLAREN: SPAIN

New front aerodynamics appeared on the McLaren in Spain, starting with the wing that was revised in all its components. The external parts of the end plates (1) were also modified; they were shorter with the interior element that protruded more at the trailing edge (2). 3) The more twisted cascade wing and the traditional unit were new (4), the latter more curved. The position of the adjustment (5) of the third element was also new and acted as a small turning vane in that area. The main plane's position was different, which forced the forward inclination (6) of the central pylons. In synergy with the new wing, these two fins were later attached to the lower part of the chassis; they integrated with the modified shape of the lower part of the nose to ensure a greater quantity of air in the lower area of the chassis. And note the numerous fins attached to the brake air intakes, with the clear task of managing the air flow in that zone.

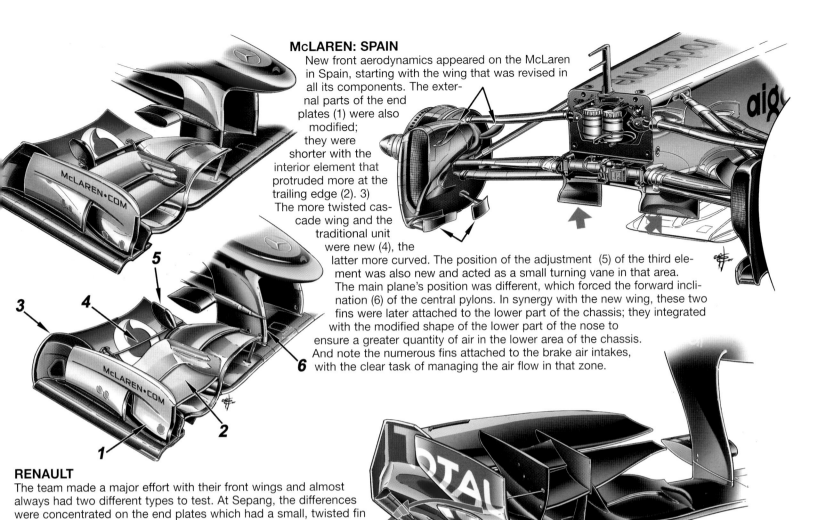

RENAULT

The team made a major effort with their front wings and almost always had two different types to test. At Sepang, the differences were concentrated on the end plates which had a small, twisted fin and a longitudinal blow, shown by the passage of air in the illustration. The principal part of the end plates was also slightly different compared to the version used in Melbourne.

FERRARI: BARCELONA

The exhaust terminals tested in Turkey on the Friday made their racing debut on the F150 Italia at Barcelona. They were linked to new lateral channels and different brake air intakes which, together with the external vertical fin, carried the hot air in the lower area of the channels, as indicated in the circle.

RED BULL: REAR WING

The McLaren and Sauber-type fringes made a double debut on the Red Bull and Ferrari at Barcelona. They were in the lower part of the end plates which, in the RB7's case, also had a squarer shape.

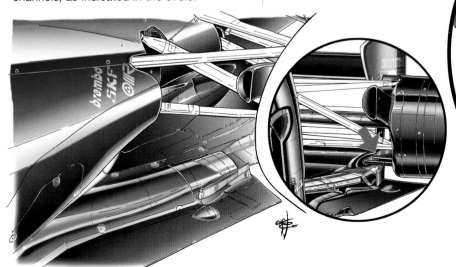

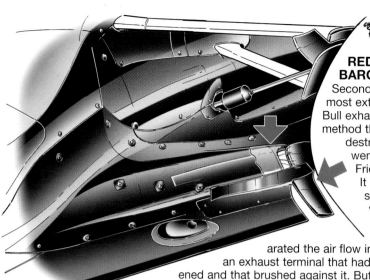

RED BULL: BARCELONA

Second test of the most extreme Red Bull exhaust blow method that Vettel had destroyed when he went off on the Friday morning. It looked like a simple small bar, but instead it was a fin integrated with the brake air intake that separated the air flow in that zone with an exhaust terminal that had been lengthened and that brushed against it. But this feature was not used in the race.

RED BULL: VALENCIA

New front aerodynamics made their first appearance in Valencia on Webber's car. The turning vanes under the central part of the nose had been removed and were replaced by two elements applied to the lower area of the chassis. This was introduced last year by Renault (below) and retained for this season's RE31. Surprisingly, this feature was re-fitted for qualifying and the race and kept for the subsequent British GP.

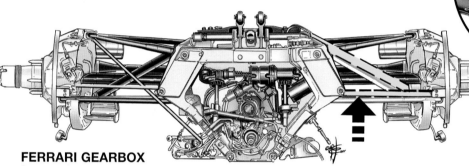

FERRARI GEARBOX

Despite problems, Ferrari decided to keep the push rod layout – shown in this illustration by the position of the rocker arm (1) – for the entire season, as well as the anti-roll bar plus, of course, the suspension mounts. The hydraulic control of the DRS can be seen at (3). Inside the carbon fibre gearbox there was an inertial damper (4) and torsion bars (5).

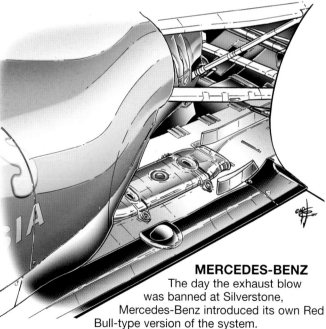

MONTREAL

New Ferrari rear suspension was tested on the Friday by Alonso. It reminded observers of the one introduced by Mercedes-Benz at Melbourne. To have a different camber recovery and a lower roll centre, the mounting point of the upper wishbone, which had become shorter and more inclined, was moved higher and inboard. The gearbox mounts were not changed, and as a result nor were the anti-squat characteristics of the suspension. On the Saturday, the team went back to the original solution as shown in the illustration. Tested again at Valencia, the system was raced at Silverstone together with a new aerodynamic package.

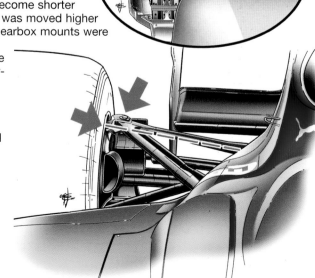

MERCEDES-BENZ

The day the exhaust blow was banned at Silverstone, Mercedes-Benz introduced its own Red Bull-type version of the system. The terminal was decidedly shorter and without the 5 cm lateral cuts in the external channel. Note the two small vertical fins to better direct the air in the upper lateral channels, which were completely covered in insulation material.

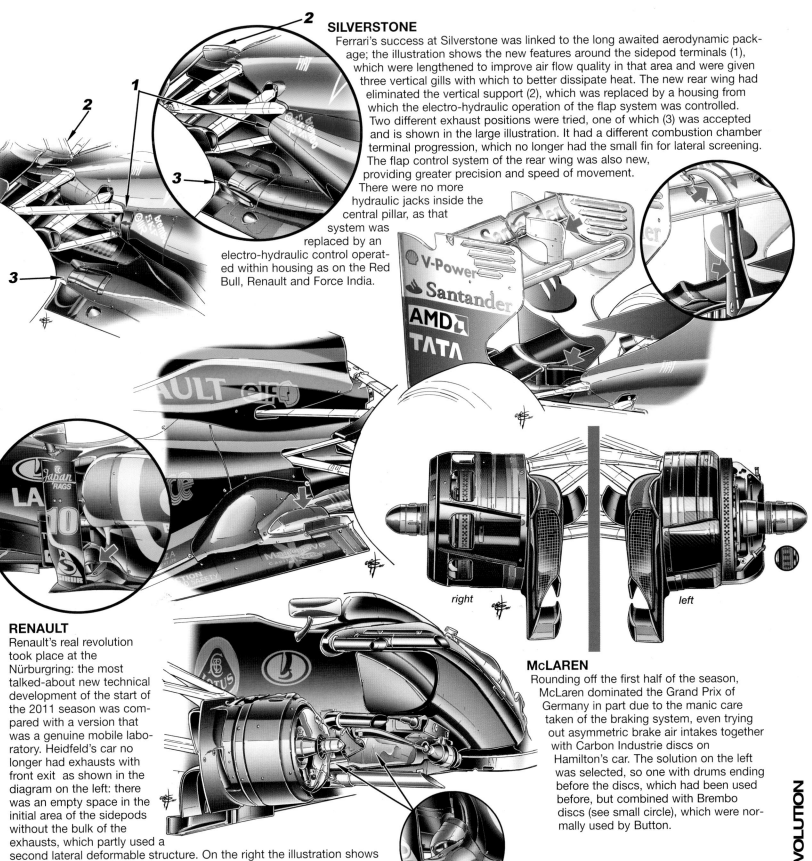

SILVERSTONE

Ferrari's success at Silverstone was linked to the long awaited aerodynamic package; the illustration shows the new features around the sidepod terminals (1), which were lengthened to improve air flow quality in that area and were given three vertical gills with which to better dissipate heat. The new rear wing had eliminated the vertical support (2), which was replaced by a housing from which the electro-hydraulic operation of the flap system was controlled. Two different exhaust positions were tried, one of which (3) was accepted and is shown in the large illustration. It had a different combustion chamber terminal progression, which no longer had the small fin for lateral screening. The flap control system of the rear wing was also new, providing greater precision and speed of movement.

There were no more hydraulic jacks inside the central pillar, as that system was replaced by an electro-hydraulic control operated within housing as on the Red Bull, Renault and Force India.

RENAULT

Renault's real revolution took place at the Nürburgring: the most talked-about new technical development of the start of the 2011 season was compared with a version that was a genuine mobile laboratory. Heidfeld's car no longer had exhausts with front exit as shown in the diagram on the left: there was an empty space in the initial area of the sidepods without the bulk of the exhausts, which partly used a second lateral deformable structure. On the right the illustration shows how the RE31 practically had no break in the so-called Coca Cola area that was similar to the other cars, in order to exploit the exhaust blow effect. Moving the exhaust terminals further worsened the situation, as can be seen in the drawing.

right

left

McLAREN

Rounding off the first half of the season, McLaren dominated the Grand Prix of Germany in part due to the manic care taken of the braking system, even trying out asymmetric brake air intakes together with Carbon Industrie discs on Hamilton's car. The solution on the left was selected, so one with drums ending before the discs, which had been used before, but combined with Brembo discs (see small circle), which were normally used by Button.

Giorgio Nada Editore Srl

Editorial manager
Leonardo Acerbi

Editorial coordination
Giorgio Nada Editore

Graphic design and cover
Aimone Bolliger

Contributors
Franco Nugnes (engines)
Ing. Giancarlo Bruno (suspensions and tyres)
Kazuhito Kasai (tyres)

Computer graphic
Alessia Bardino
Belinda Lucid
Camillo Morande
Elena Cerro
Gisella Nicosia
Marco Verna
Paolo Rondelli

3D animations
Camillo Morande
Generoso Annunziata

Printed in Italy by
Grafiche Flaminia Srl
Foligno (PG)
september 2011

© 2011 Giorgio Nada Editore, Vimodrone (Milan, Italy)

The catalogue of Giorgio Nada Editore publications is available on request at the address below.

Giorgio Nada Editore
Via Claudio Treves,15/17
I - 20090 VIMODRONE MI
Tel. +39 02 27301126
Fax +39 02 27301454
e-mail: info@giorgionadaeditore.it
www.giorgionadaeditore.it

Distribution
Giunti Editore Spa
via Bolognese 165
I - 50139 FIRENZE
www.giunti.it

Formula 1 2010-2011 - technical analysis
ISBN 978-88-7911-526-1